Second Edition

The Pocket Handbook

for

History

LAURIE G. KIRSZNER
University of the Sciences in Philadelphia

STEPHEN R. MANDELL
Drexel University

with

JESSIE SWIGGER
University of Texas at Austin

Contributing Editor: PATRICK BIZZARO
East Carolina University

THOMSON
WADSWORTH

Australia   Canada   Mexico   Singapore   Spain   United Kingdom   United States

THOMSON
*
WADSWORTH ™

The Pocket Handbook for History
Laurie G. Kirszner, Stephen R. Mandell

Publisher: *Michael Rosenberg*
Acquisitions Editor: *Dickson Musselwhite*
Development Editor: *Karen Judd*
Production Editor: *Maryellen Eschmann-Killeen*
Director of HED Marketing: *Lisa Kimball*
Marketing Manager: *Katrina Byrd*
Manufacturing Coordinator: *Mary Beth Hennebury*
Text Designer, Compositor: *Thompson Steele, Inc.*
Project Manager: *Andrea Fincke*
Cover Designer: *Diane Levy*
Printer: *RR Donnelley and Sons*

Printed in the United States of America.
1 2 3 4 5 6 7 8 9 10   07 06 05 04 03

For more information contact Heinle, 25 Thomson Place, Boston, Massachusetts 02210 USA, or you can visit our Internet site at
http://www.heinle.com

ISBN: 0-759-39610-8 (Standard Edition)
ISBN: 0-534-55853-4 (InfoTrac® Edition)

Library of Congress Control Number: 2003111638

PREFACE

We would like to introduce you to *The Pocket Handbook for History*, a quick reference guide for college students. This book was designed to be a truly portable handbook that will easily fit in a backpack or pocket yet can serve as a valuable resource. Despite its compact size, however, *The Pocket Handbook for History* offers coverage of all the topics that you would expect to find in a much longer book: the writing process (including a model student paper); sentence grammar and style; punctuation and mechanics; the research process (including two complete model student research papers); and Chicago documentation style. In addition, the book devotes a full section to practical assignments (including document and Web page design, writing for the workplace, and making oral presentations) as well as an appendix that addresses concerns facing ESL students. Thus, the book's explanations and examples of writing can guide college students not just in first-year courses, but throughout their college careers and beyond.

In preparing *The Pocket Handbook for History,* we focused on making the book inviting, useful, clear, and—most of all—easy to navigate. To achieve these goals, we incorporated distinctive design features throughout that make information easy to find and easy to use.

- A color-coded guide to the nine parts of the book appears on the back cover. Inside the book, the pages of each part are marked by a distinctive color bar that corresponds to a color on this guide.
- A brief table of contents is provided inside the front cover. Here too, the parts are color-coded to link them with the corresponding sections of the text.
- Close-up boxes that focus on special problems are identified by a magnifying glass icon.
- Checklists for quick reference are distinguished by a checkmark icon.
- A computer icon identifies information that students will need as they write and revise.
- Boxed lists and charts set off other information that students are likely to refer to on a regular basis.
- Marginal cross-references (keyed to blue, underlined terms in the text) direct students to related discussions in other parts of the book.

Preface

To make it useful to students, the book includes the following features:

- A four-chapter research section, including complete coverage of the research process, using and evaluating library sources, using and evaluating Internet sources, and integrating sources and avoiding plagiarism
- A CMS paper, "Forgotten Heroes: The Buffalo Soldiers"
- Thorough, up-to-date coverage of Chicago style (The Chicago Manual of Style, 15th ed.), with special attention to documenting electronic sources
- A chapter on writing for the workplace (including discussions of résumés, letters of application, memos, and e-mail)
- Coverage of Web page design along with document design
- A chapter on making oral presentations

With the publication of *The Pocket Handbook for History*, the *Wadsworth Handbook* series consists of three general handbooks: *The Wadsworth Handbook*, for those who want a full-size, comprehensive reference book with exercises; *The Brief Handbook*, for those who want a compact, tabbed reference guide; and *The Pocket Handbook*, for those who want a concise, portable reference. In addition, there are the various discipline-specific *Pocket Handbooks*—such as this book, *The Pocket Handbook for History*—for those who want a concise guide for writing in the humanities, social sciences, or natural sciences.

In all the different versions of the *Wadsworth Handbook* series, our goal is the same: to give students the guidance they need to become self-reliant writers and to succeed in college and beyond. Helping us to achieve these goals has been an extraordinary team at Wadsworth: Camille Adkins, Julie McBurney, Michael Rosenberg, Dickson Musselwhite, Karen Judd, and Lianne Ames. We are also indebted to production editors Maryellen Eschmann-Killeen and Andrea Fincke and to Pat Bizzaro of East Carolina University and Jesse Swigger of the University of Texas at Austin. We are very grateful for all this help and support, and grateful as well to our families for their continued patience and enthusiasm.

Laurie G. Kirszner
Stephen R. Mandell

CONTENTS

Contents

Contents

Contents

Contents

INFOTRAC®
COLLEGE EDITION
The Online Library

A FREE 4-month Access Card for *InfoTrac® College Edition* comes with every new copy of Kirszner and Mandell, *The Pocket Handbook for History*. Indispensable when writing research papers, *InfoTrac® College Edition* offers students 24-hour-a-day access to a database of over 10 million full-length articles from hundreds of scholarly and popular periodicals.

PART 1

WRITING ESSAYS AND PARAGRAPHS

CHAPTER 1

WRITING ESSAYS

Writing is a constant process of decision making—of selecting, deleting, and rearranging material.

THE WRITING PROCESS

Planning: Consider your purpose, audience, and assignment; choose a topic; discover ideas to write about.
Shaping: Decide how to organize your material.
Drafting: Write your first draft.
Revising: "Re-see" what you have written; write additional drafts.
Editing: Check grammar, spelling, punctuation, and mechanics.
Proofreading: Check for typographical errors.

1a Understanding Essay Structure

The essays you write for your college courses will have a thesis-and-support structure. A **thesis-and-support essay** includes a **thesis statement** (which expresses the **thesis,** or main idea, of the essay) and the specific information that explains and develops that thesis. Your essay will consist of several paragraphs: an **introductory paragraph**, which introduces your thesis; a See **concluding paragraph**, which gives your essay a sense of completion, perhaps restating your thesis; and a number of **body paragraphs,** which provide the support for your essay's thesis. 2d1-2

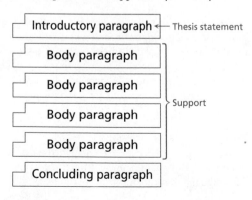

- Introductory paragraph ← Thesis statement
- Body paragraph
- Body paragraph
- Body paragraph } Support
- Body paragraph
- Concluding paragraph

1b Writing Effective Thesis Statements

An effective thesis statement has four characteristics.

1. *An effective thesis statement should clearly communicate your essay's main idea.* It tells your readers not only what your essay's topic is, but also how you will approach that topic and what you will say about it. Thus, your thesis statement reflects your essay's purpose.

2. *An effective thesis statement should be more than a general subject, a statement of fact, or an announcement of your intent.*

   SUBJECT: Intelligence tests

   STATEMENT OF FACT: Intelligence tests are used for placement in many elementary schools.

   ANNOUNCEMENT: The essay that follows will show that intelligence tests may be inaccurate.

   THESIS STATEMENT: Although intelligence tests are widely used for placement in many elementary schools, they are not the best measure of a student's academic performance.

3. *An effective thesis statement should be carefully worded.* Your thesis statement—usually expressed in a single, concise sentence—should be direct and straightforward. Avoid vague phrases, such as *centers on, deals with, involves, revolves around,* or *is concerned with.* Do not include phrases like *As I will show, I plan to demonstrate,* and *It seems to me,* which weaken your credibility by suggesting that your conclusions are based on opinion rather than on reading, observation, and experience.

4. *Finally, an effective thesis statement should suggest your essay's direction, emphasis, and scope.* Your thesis statement should not make promises that your essay will not fulfill. It should suggest the major points you will cover, the order in which you will introduce them, and where you will place your emphasis, as the following thesis statement does.

   EFFECTIVE THESIS STATEMENT: Widely ridiculed as escape reading, romance novels are becoming increasingly important as a proving ground for many first-time writers and, more significantly, as a showcase for strong heroines.

NOTE: As you write and rewrite, you may modify your essay's direction, emphasis, and scope; if you do so, you must reword your thesis statement.

1c Drafting and Revising

(1) Writing a Rough Draft

When you write a rough draft, you get ideas down on paper so you can react to them. You will generally write several drafts of your essay, and you should expect to add or delete words, to reword sentences, to rethink ideas, to reorder paragraphs—even to take an unexpected detour that may lead you to a new perspective on your topic. To make revision easier, leave room on the page so that you can add material or rewrite. If you type, triple-space; if you write by hand, skip lines. To streamline your revision process, use symbols (arrows, circles, boxes, numbers, and so on) that signal various operations to you.

(2) Revising Your Drafts

Everyone's revision process is different, but the following specific strategies can be helpful at this stage of the process.

- **Outline your draft.** An outline can help you check the logic of your paper's structure.
- **Do collaborative revision.** Ask a friend to give you feedback on your draft.
- **Use instructors' comments.** Study written comments on your draft, and arrange a conference if necessary.
- **Use revision checklists.** Revise in stages, first looking at the whole essay and then considering the paragraphs, sentences, and words. Use the revision checklists that follow to guide you through the process.

✔ CHECKLIST: REVISING THE WHOLE ESSAY

- ✔ Are thesis and support logically related, with each body paragraph supporting one aspect of your thesis statement? **(See 1b)**
- ✔ Is your thesis statement clearly and specifically worded? **(See 1c)**
- ✔ Have you discussed everything promised in your thesis statement? **(See 1c)**

✔ CHECKLIST: REVISING PARAGRAPHS

- ✔ Does each body paragraph focus on one main idea, expressed in a clearly worded topic sentence? **(See 2a)**
- ✔ Are the relationships of sentences within paragraphs clear? **(See 2b)**
- ✔ Are your body paragraphs fully developed? **(See 2c)**
- ✔ Does your introductory paragraph arouse interest and prepare readers for what is to come? **(See 2d1)**
- ✔ Does your concluding paragraph review your main points? **(See 2d2)**

✔ CHECKLIST: REVISING SENTENCES

- ✔ Have you used correct sentence structure? **(See Chapters 3 and 4)**
- ✔ Are your sentences varied? **(See Chapter 9)**
- ✔ Have you eliminated nonessential words and unnecessary repetition? **(See 10a–b)**
- ✔ Have you avoided overloading your sentences with too many clauses? **(See 10c)**
- ✔ Have you avoided potentially confusing shifts in tense, voice, mood, person, or number? **(See 11a)**
- ✔ Are your sentences constructed logically? **(See 11b–c)**
- ✔ Have you strengthened sentences with repetition, balance, and parallelism? **(See 12a)**
- ✔ Have you placed modifiers clearly and logically? **(See Chapter 13)**

✔ CHECKLIST: REVISING WORDS

- ✔ Have you eliminated jargon, pretentious diction, clichés, and biased language from your writing? **(See 14a–d)**

CHOOSING A TITLE

- A title should convey your essay's focus, perhaps using key words and phrases from your essay or echoing the wording of your assignment.
- A title should arouse interest, perhaps with a provocative question, a quotation, or a controversial position.

ASSIGNMENT: Write about a problem faced on college campuses today.

TOPIC: Free speech on campus

POSSIBLE TITLES:

Free Speech: A Problem for Today's Colleges (echoes wording of assignment and uses key words of essay)

How Free Should Free Speech on Campus Be? (provocative question)

The Right to "Shout 'Fire' in a Crowded Theater" (quotation)

Hate Speech: A Dangerous Abuse of Free Speech on Campus (controversial position)

Editing and Proofreading

When you **edit,** you concentrate on grammar, spelling, punctuation, and mechanics. When you **proofread,** you reread every word carefully to make sure you did not make any errors as you typed.

 EDITING AND PROOFREADING

- As you edit, look at only a small portion of text at a time. If your software allows you to split the screen, create another window so small that you can see only one or two lines of text at a time.
- Use the *search* or *find* command to look for words or phrases in usage errors that you commonly make—for instance, confusing *it's* with *its*. You can also uncover **sexist language** by searching for words such as *he, his, him,* or *man*.

See
14d2

continued on the following page

continued from the previous page

- Remember that a spell checker will not catch a typo that creates a correctly spelled word—for example, *there* for *their* or *form* for *from*. Even after you run a spell check, you still must proofread your papers carefully.

1e Model Student Paper

Masterton 1

Samantha Masterton

Professor Wade

English 101

15 November 2002

Title

The Returning Student:

Older Is Definitely Better

After graduating from high school, young people must decide what they want to do with the rest of their lives. Many graduates (often without much thought) decide to continue their education in college. This group of teenagers makes up what many see as the typical first-year college student. Recently, however, this stereotype has been challenged by an influx of older students into American colleges and universities. My experience as one

Thesis statement

of these older students has convinced me that many students would benefit from taking a few years off between high school and college.

First point in support of thesis

The college experience of an eighteen-year-old is quite different from that of an older student. Teenagers are often concerned with things other than cracking books—

Model Student Paper

going to parties, dating, and testing personal limits, for example. I almost never see older students cutting lectures or wasting time as younger students do. Most older students have saved for tuition and want to get their money's worth. Many are also balancing the demands of home and work to attend classes, so they know how important it is to do well.

Generally, young people just out of high school have not learned how to set priorities or meet deadlines. Younger college students often find themselves hopelessly behind or scrambling at the last minute simply because they have not learned how to budget their time. Although success in college depends on the ability to set realistic goals and organize time and materials, college itself does little to help students develop these skills. On the contrary, the workplace—where reward and punishment are usually immediate and tangible—is the best place to learn such lessons. Working teaches the basics that college takes for granted: the value of

Second point in support of thesis

---

punctuality and attendance, the importance of respect for superiors and colleagues, and the need for establishing priorities and meeting deadlines.

The adult student who has gained experience in the workplace has advantages over the younger student. In general, the older student enrolls in college with a definite course of study in mind. For the adult student, college is an extension of work rather than a place to discover what

Third point in support of thesis

work will be. This greater sense of purpose makes older students more focused and more highly motivated.

Fourth point in support of thesis

Because of their age and greater experience, older students bring more into the classroom than younger students do. Eighteen-year-olds have been driving for only a year or two; they have just gotten the right to vote; and they usually have not lived on their own. In contrast, older students have generally had a good deal of life experience. This experience enables them to make significant contributions to class discussions and group projects, and it enriches their written work as well. Moreover, their

Masterton 4

years in the real world have helped them to become more focused and more responsible than they were when they graduated from high school. As a result, they are better prepared for college. Thus, they not only bring more into the classroom but also take more out of it.

Conclusion

All things considered, higher education is often wasted on the young, who are either too immature or too unfocused to take advantage of it. Many older students have taken time off to serve in the military, to get a job, or to raise a family. Many have traveled, read widely, engaged in informal study, and taken the time to grow up. By the time they get to college, they have defined their goals and made a commitment to achieve them. Taking a few years off between high school and college would give younger students the breathing room they need to make the most of college. It would also give them the life experience they need to appreciate the value of their education.

CHAPTER 2

WRITING PARAGRAPHS

A **paragraph** is a group of related sentences. It may be complete in itself or part of a longer piece of writing.

✔ CHECKLIST: WHEN TO PARAGRAPH

- ✔ Begin a new paragraph whenever you move from one major point to another.
- ✔ Begin a new paragraph whenever you move your readers from one time period or location to another.
- ✔ Begin a new paragraph whenever you introduce a new step in a process or sequence.
- ✔ Begin a new paragraph when you want to emphasize an important idea.
- ✔ Begin a new paragraph every time a new person speaks.
- ✔ Begin a new paragraph to signal the end of your introduction and the beginning of your conclusion.

2a Writing Unified Paragraphs

A paragraph is **unified** when it develops a single idea. Each paragraph should have a **topic sentence** that states the main idea of the paragraph; the other sentences in the paragraph support that idea.

<u>I was a listening child, careful to hear the very different sounds of Spanish and English.</u> Wide-eyed with hearing, I'd listen to sounds more than words. First, there were English (*gringo*) sounds. So many words were still unknown that when the butcher or the lady at the drugstore said something to me, exotic polysyllabic sounds would bloom in the midst of their sentences. Often the speech of people in public seemed to me very loud, booming with confidence. The man behind the counter would literally ask, "What can I do for you?" But by being so firm and so clear, the sound of his voice said that he was a *gringo*; he belonged in public society. (Richard Rodriguez, *Aria: A Memoir of a Bilingual Childhood*)

Topic sentence

Support

2b Writing Coherent Paragraphs

A paragraph is **coherent** when all its sentences are logically related to one another. **Transitional words and phrases** clarify the relationships among sentences by establishing the spatial, chronological, and logical connections within a paragraph.

Topic sentence
Transitional words and phrases (*after, finally,* and so on) establish chronology of events.

Napoleon certainly made a change for the worse by leaving his small kingdom of Elba. <u>After Waterloo</u>, he went back to Paris, and he abdicated for a second time. <u>A hundred days after</u> his return from Elba, he fled to Rochefort in hope of escaping to America. <u>Finally</u>, he gave himself up to the English captain of the ship *Bellerophon*. <u>Once again</u>, he suggested that the Prince Regent grant him asylum, and <u>once again</u>, he was refused. <u>In the end</u>, all he saw of England was the Devon coast and Plymouth Sound as he passed on to the remote island of St. Helena. <u>After six years of exile</u>, he died on May 5, 1821, at the age of fifty-two. (Norman Mackenzie, *The Escape from Elba*)

USING TRANSITIONAL WORDS AND PHRASES

To Signal Sequence or Addition
again, also, besides, furthermore, moreover, in addition, first . . . second . . . third, one . . . another, too

To Signal Time
afterward, as soon as, at first, at the same time, before, earlier, finally, in the meantime, later, meanwhile, next, now, since, soon, subsequently, then, until

To Signal Comparison
also, by the same token, likewise, in comparison, similarly

To Signal Contrast
although, but, despite, even though, however, in contrast, instead, meanwhile, nevertheless, nonetheless, on the contrary, on the one hand . . . on the other hand, still, whereas, yet

To Introduce Examples
for example, for instance, namely, specifically, thus

continued on the following page

---

continued from the previous page

To Signal Narrowing of Focus
after all, indeed, in fact, in other words, in particular, specifically, that is

To Introduce Conclusions or Summaries
as a result, consequently, in summary, therefore, in conclusion, in other words, thus, to conclude

To Signal Concession
admittedly, certainly, granted, naturally, of course

To Introduce Causes or Effects
accordingly, as a result, because, consequently, hence, since, so, then, therefore

NOTE: <u>Parallel</u> constructions ("He was a patriot. . . . He was a reformer. . . . He was an innovator. . . .") and repeated key words and phrases ("He invented a new type of printing press. . . . This printing press. . . .") also help writers achieve coherence. _{See 12a}

2c Writing Well-Developed Paragraphs

A paragraph is **well developed** when it contains all the support—examples, statistics, expert opinion, and so on—that readers need to understand the main idea.

From Thanksgiving until Christmas, children are bombarded with ads for violent toys and games. Toy manufacturers persist in thinking that only toys that appeal to children's aggressiveness will sell. <u>One television commercial praises the merits of a commando team that attacks and captures a miniature enemy base. Toy soldiers wear realistic uniforms and carry automatic rifles, pistols, knives, grenades, and ammunition. Another commercial shows laughing children shooting one another with plastic rocket fighters and tank-like vehicles.</u> Despite claims that they (unlike action toys) have educational value, video games have increased the level of violence. <u>The most popular video games involve children in strikingly realistic combat situations. One game lets children search out and destroy enemy fighters in outer space. Other best-selling games graphically simulate hand-to-hand combat on city streets.</u> The real question is why parents buy these violent toys and games for their children. (Student Writer)

Topic sentence

Specific examples

Specific examples

2d Writing Introductory and Concluding Paragraphs

(1) Introductory Paragraphs

An **introductory paragraph** introduces the subject, narrows it, and then states the essay's thesis.

> Although it has now faded from view, the telegraph lives on within the communications technologies that have subsequently built upon its foundations: the telephone, the fax machine, and, more recently, the Internet. <u>And, ironically, it is the Internet—despite being regarded as a quintessentially modern means of communication—that has the most in common with its telegraphic ancestor.</u> (Tom Standage, *The Victorian Internet*)

Thesis statement (margin label)

An introductory paragraph may arouse readers' interest with an interesting quotation, a compelling question, an unusual comparison, or a controversial statement.

NOTE: Avoid introductions that simply announce your subject ("In my paper I will talk about Lady Macbeth") or that undercut your credibility ("I don't know much about alternative energy sources, but I would like to present my opinion").

✔ CHECKLIST: REVISING INTRODUCTIONS

- ✔ Does your introduction include your essay's thesis statement?
- ✔ Does it lead naturally into the body of your essay?
- ✔ Does it arouse your readers' interest?
- ✔ Does it avoid statements that simply announce your subject or that undercut your credibility?

---

(2) Concluding Paragraphs

A **concluding paragraph** typically begins with specifics—for example, a review of the essay's main points—and then moves to more general statements.

> As an Arab-American, I feel I have the best of two worlds. I'm proud to be part of the melting pot, proud to contribute to the tremendous diversity of cultures, customs and traditions that make this country unique. But Arab-bashing—public acceptance of hatred and bigotry—is something no American can be proud of. (Ellen Mansoor Collier, "I Am Not a Terrorist")

A concluding paragraph may also offer a prediction, a recommendation, a forceful opinion, or a pertinent quotation.

NOTE: Avoid conclusions that just repeat your introduction in different words or that cast doubt on your concluding points ("I may not be an expert" or "At least this is my opinion"). If possible, end with a statement that readers will remember.

✔ CHECKLIST: REVISING CONCLUSIONS

✔ Does your conclusion sum up your essay, perhaps by reviewing the essay's main points?
✔ Does it do more than just repeat the introduction?
✔ Does it avoid apologies?
✔ Does it end memorably?

PART 2

WRITING GRAMMATICAL SENTENCES

CHAPTER 3

REVISING COMMA SPLICES AND FUSED SENTENCES

A **run-on sentence** is created when two <u>independent clauses</u> are joined incorrectly. See A2.3

A **comma splice** is a run-on that occurs when two independent clauses are joined by just a comma. A **fused sentence** is a run-on that occurs when two independent clauses are joined with no punctuation.

> **COMMA SPLICE:** Charles Dickens created the character of Mr. Micawber, he also created Uriah Heep.

> **FUSED SENTENCE:** Charles Dickens created the character of Mr. Micawber he also created Uriah Heep.

✔ CHECKLIST: REVISING COMMA SPLICES AND FUSED SENTENCES

To revise a comma splice or fused sentence, use one of the following strategies.

✔ Add a period between the clauses.
✔ Add a semicolon between the clauses.
✔ Add an appropriate coordinating conjunction.
✔ Subordinate one clause to the other, creating a complex sentence.

3a Revising with Periods

You can add a period between the independent clauses, creating two separate sentences. This is a good strategy to use when the clauses are long or when they are not closely related.

In 1894 Frenchman Alfred Dreyfus was falsely convicted of treason, His struggle for justice pitted the army against the civil libertarians.

3b   Revising with Semicolons

See 17a   You can add a **semicolon** between two closely related clauses that convey parallel or constrasting information.

Chippendale chairs have straight legs; however, Queen Anne chairs have curved legs.

See 2b   **NOTE:** When you use a **transitional word or phrase** (such as *however, therefore,* or *for example*) to connect two independent clauses, the transitional element must be preceded by a semicolon and followed by a comma. If you use a comma alone, you create a comma splice. If you omit punctuation entirely, you create a fused sentence.

3c   Revising with Coordinating Conjunctions

You can use a coordinating conjunction (*and, or, but, nor, for, so, yet*) to join two closely related clauses of equal importance into one **compound sentence**. The coordinating conjunction you choose indicates the relationship between the clauses: addition (*and*), contrast (*but, yet*), causality (*for, so*), or a choice of alternatives (*or, nor*). Be sure to add a comma before the coordinating conjunction.

See 9a1

Elias Howe invented the sewing machine, *and* Julia Ward Howe was a poet and social reformer.

3d   Revising with Subordinating Conjunctions or Relative Pronouns

When the ideas in two independent clauses are not of equal importance, you can use an appropriate subordinating conjunction or a relative pronoun to join the clauses into one **complex sentence**, placing the less important idea in the dependent clause.

See 9a2

Stravinsky's ballet *The Rite of Spring* shocked Parisians in 1913, *because* its rhythms seemed erotic.

Lady Mary Wortley Montagu, *who* had suffered from smallpox herself, ~~she~~ helped spread the practice of inoculation.

CHAPTER 4

REVISING SENTENCE FRAGMENTS

A **sentence fragment** is an incomplete sentence—a clause or a phrase—that is punctuated as though it were a sentence. A sentence may be incomplete for any of the following reasons.

- It lacks a subject.

  Many astrophysicists now believe that galaxies are distributed in clusters. <u>And even form supercluster complexes.</u>

- It lacks a verb.

  Every generation has its defining moments. <u>Usually the events with the most news coverage.</u>

- It lacks both a subject and a verb.

  Researchers are engaged in a variety of studies. <u>Suggesting a link between alcoholism and heredity.</u> (*Suggesting* is a **verbal**, which cannot serve as a sentence's main verb.)   See A1.3

- It is a **dependent clause**, a clause that begins with a subordinating conjunction or relative pronoun.   See A2.3

  Bishop Desmond Tutu was awarded the 1984 Nobel Peace Prize. <u>Because he struggled to end apartheid.</u>

  The pH meter and the spectrophotometer are two scientific instruments. <u>That changed the chemistry laboratory dramatically.</u>

 CLOSE-UP

MAINTAINING SENTENCE BOUNDARIES

When readers cannot see where sentences begin and end, they have difficulty understanding what you have written. For instance, it is impossible to tell to which independent clause the fragment in each of the following sequences belongs.

The course requirements were changed last year. <u>Because a new professor was hired at the very end of the spring semester.</u> I was unable to find out about this change until after preregistration.

✔ CHECKLIST: REVISING SENTENCE FRAGMENTS

To revise a sentence fragment, use one or more of the following strategies.

✔ Attach the fragment to an adjacent independent clause that contains the missing words.
✔ Delete the subordinating conjunction or relative pronoun.
✔ Supply the missing subject or verb (or both).

4a Attaching the Fragment to an Independent Clause

In most cases, the simplest way to correct a fragment is by attaching it to an adjacent independent clause that contains the missing words.

President Johnson did not seek reelection. ~~For~~ for a number of reasons. (**prepositional phrase** fragment)

See A2.3

Students sometimes take a leave of absence. ~~To~~ to decide on definite career goals. (**verbal phrase** fragment)

See A2.3

The pilot changed course. ~~Realizing~~ , realizing that the weather was worsening. (verbal phrase fragment)

Brian was the star forward of the Blue Devils. ~~The~~ , the team with the most wins. (**appositive** fragment)

See 7b3

Fairy tales are full of damsels in distress. ~~Such~~ , such as Rapunzel. (appositive fragment)

People with dyslexia have trouble reading. ~~And~~ and may also find it difficult to write. (part of compound predicate)

They took only a compass and a canteen. ~~And~~ and some trail mix. (part of compound object)

Property taxes rose sharply. ~~Although~~ although city services declined. (**dependent clause** fragment)

See A2.3

The battery is dead, which ~~Which~~ means the car won't start.

(dependent clause fragment)

REVISING SENTENCE FRAGMENTS: LISTS

When a fragment takes the form of a **list**, add a colon to connect the list to the independent clause that introduces it.

See 25a1

Tourists often outnumber residents in four European cities: ~~,~~ Venice, Florence, Canterbury, and Bath.

4b Deleting the Subordinating Conjunction or Relative Pronoun

When a fragment consists of a dependent clause that is punctuated as though it were a complete sentence, you can correct it by attaching it to an adjacent independent clause, as illustrated in **4a.** Alternatively, you can simply delete the subordinating conjunction or relative pronoun.

Property taxes rose sharply. ~~Although city~~ City services declined.

(subordinating conjunction *although* deleted)

The battery is dead. ~~Which~~ This means the car won't start. (relative pronoun *which* replaced by *this,* a word that can serve as the sentence's subject)

NOTE: Simply deleting the subordinating conjunction or relative pronoun is usually the least desirable way to revise a sentence fragment. It is likely to create two choppy sentences and obscure the connection between them.

REVISING SENTENCE FRAGMENTS

Sentence fragments are often used in speech and in e-mail as well as in journalism, advertising, and creative writing. In most college writing situations, however, sentence fragments are not acceptable. Do not use them without carefully considering their suitability for your audience and purpose.

4c   Supplying the Missing Subject or Verb

Another way to correct a fragment is to add the missing words (a subject or a verb or both) that are needed to make the fragment a sentence.

                  It was divided

In 1948, India became independent. ~~Divided~~ into the nations

of India and Pakistan. (verbal phrase fragment)

                         It reminds

A familiar trademark can increase a product's sales. ~~Reminding~~

shoppers that the product has a long-standing reputation.

(verbal phrase fragment)

CHAPTER 5

UNDERSTANDING AGREEMENT

Agreement is the correspondence between words in number, gender, or person. Subjects and verbs agree in **number** (singular or plural) and **person** (first, second, or third); pronouns and their antecedents agree in number, person, and **gender**.

See 11a4

5a Making Subjects and Verbs Agree

Singular subjects take singular verbs, and plural subjects take plural verbs. **Present tense** verbs, except *be* and *have*, add -*s* or -*es* when the subject is third-person singular. (Third-person singular subjects include nouns; the personal pronouns *he, she, it,* and *one*; and many **indefinite pronouns**.)

See 6b1

See 5a4

The <u>President</u> <u>has</u> the power to veto congressional legislation.

<u>She</u> frequently <u>cites</u> statistics to support her points.

In every group <u>somebody</u> <u>emerges</u> as a natural leader.

Present tense verbs do not add -*s* or -*es* when the subject is a plural noun, a first-person or second-person pronoun (*I, we, you*), or a third-person plural pronoun (*they*).

<u>Experts</u> <u>recommend</u> that dieters avoid processed meat.

At this stratum, <u>we</u> <u>see</u> rocks dating back ten million years.

<u>They</u> <u>say</u> that some wealthy people default on their student loans.

In some situations, making subjects and verbs agree can be troublesome.

(1) Words Between Subject and Verb

If a modifying phrase comes between the subject and the verb, the verb should agree with the subject, not with a word in the modifying phrase.

The <u>sound</u> of the drumbeats <u>builds</u> in intensity in *The Emperor Jones.*

The <u>games</u> won by the intramural team <u>are</u> few and far between.

This rule also applies to phrases introduced by *along with, as well as, in addition to, including,* and *together with.*

Heavy <u>rain</u>, along with high winds, <u>causes</u> hazardous driving conditions.

(2) Compound Subjects Joined by *and*

Compound subjects joined by *and* usually take plural verbs.

<u>Air bags and antilock brakes</u> <u>are</u> standard on all new models.

There are, however, two exceptions to this rule. First, compound subjects joined by *and* that stand for a single idea or person are treated as a unit and used with singular verbs: <u>Rhythm and blues</u> <u>is</u> a forerunner of rock and roll.

Second, when *each* or *every* precedes a compound subject joined by *and,* the subject takes a singular verb: <u>Every desk and file cabinet</u> <u>was</u> searched before the letter was found.

(3) Compound Subjects Joined by *or*

Compound subjects joined by *or* may take singular or plural verbs. If both subjects are singular, use a singular verb; if both are plural, use a plural verb. If a singular and a plural subject are linked by *or* (or by *either . . . or, neither . . . nor,* or *not only . . . but also*), the verb agrees with the subject that is nearer to it.

<u>Either radiation treatments or chemotherapy</u> <u>is</u> combined with surgery for effective results.

<u>Either chemotherapy or radiation treatments</u> <u>are</u> combined with surgery for effective results.

(4) Indefinite Pronouns

Some **indefinite pronouns**—*both, many, few, several, others*—are always plural and take plural verbs. Most others—*another, anyone, everyone, one, each, either, neither, anything, everything, something, nothing, nobody,* and *somebody*—are singular and take singular verbs.

<u>Anyone</u> <u>is</u> welcome to apply for the scholarship.

<u>Each</u> of the chapters <u>includes</u> a review exercise.

A few indefinite pronouns—*some, all, any, more, most,* and *none*—can be singular or plural, depending on the noun they

...le <u>is</u> to be expected. (*Some* refers to *trouble.*)

...rs <u>are</u> restless. (*Some* refers to *spectators.*)

25

...s *with, as*

...uns

...ames a group of persons or things—for
...*association, band.* When it refers to the

group as a unit (as it usually does), a collective noun takes a singular verb; when it refers to the individuals or items that make up the group, it takes a plural verb.

To many people, the <u>royal family symbolizes</u> Great Britain. (The family, as a unit, is the symbol.)

The <u>family</u> all <u>eat</u> at different times. (Each member eats separately.)

Phrases that name fixed amounts—*three quarters, twenty dollars, the majority*—are treated like collective nouns. When the amount denotes a unit, it takes a singular verb; when it denotes parts of the whole, it takes a plural verb.

<u>Three quarters</u> of his usual salary <u>is</u> not enough to live on.

<u>Three quarters</u> of the patients <u>improve</u> dramatically after treatment.

(6) Singular Subjects With Plural Forms

A singular subject takes a singular verb, even if the form of the subject is plural.

<u>Statistics</u> <u>deals</u> with the collection and analysis of data.

When such a word has a plural meaning, however, use a plural verb.

The <u>statistics</u> <u>prove</u> him wrong.

(7) Inverted Subject-Verb Order

Even when the verb comes before the subject (as it does in questions and in sentences beginning with *there is* or *there are*), the subject and verb must agree.

<u>Is</u> <u>either</u> answer correct?

There <u>are</u> currently thirteen circuit <u>courts</u> of appeals in the federal system.

(8) Linking Verbs

A **linking verb** should agree with its subject, not with the subject complement. ^{See 8a}

The <u>problem</u> <u>was</u> termites.

<u>Termites</u> <u>were</u> the problem.

(9) Relative Pronouns

When you use a **relative pronoun** (*who, which, that,* and so on) to introduce a dependent clause, the verb in the dependent clause should agree in number with the pronoun's **antecedent,** the word to which the pronoun refers. ^{See A1.2}

27

The farmer is among the <u>ones</u> who <u>suffer</u> during a grain embargo.

The farmer is the only <u>one</u> who <u>suffers</u> during a grain embargo.

5b Making Pronouns and Antecedents Agree

Singular pronouns—such as *he, him, she, her, it, me, myself,* and *oneself*—should refer to singular antecedents. Plural pronouns—such as *we, us, they, them,* and *their*—should refer to plural antecedents.

(1) Compound Antecedents

In most cases, use a plural pronoun to refer to a **compound antecedent** (two or more antecedents connected by *and*).

<u>Mormonism and Christian Science</u> were similar in <u>their</u> beginnings.

Use a singular pronoun when a compound antecedent is preceded by *each* or *every.*

<u>Every programming language and software package</u> has <u>its</u> limitations.

Use a singular pronoun to refer to two or more singular antecedents linked by *or* or *nor.*

<u>Neither Thoreau nor Whitman</u> lived to see <u>his</u> work read widely.

When one part of a compound antecedent is singular and one part is plural, the pronoun agrees in person and number with the antecedent that is nearer to it.

<u>Neither the boy nor his parents</u> had <u>their</u> seatbelts fastened.

(2) Collective Noun Antecedents

If the meaning of a collective noun antecedent is singular (as it will be in most cases), use a singular pronoun. If the meaning is plural, use a plural pronoun.

The teachers' <u>union</u> announced <u>its</u> plan to strike. (The members act as a unit.)

The <u>team</u> moved to <u>their</u> positions. (Each member acts individually.)

(3) Indefinite Pronoun Antecedents

Most <u>**indefinite pronouns**</u>—*each, either, neither, one, anyone,* and the like—are singular and are used with singular pronouns.

See 5a4

<u>Neither</u> of the men had <u>his</u> proposal ready by the deadline.

<u>Each</u> of these neighborhoods has <u>its</u> own traditions and values.

(A few indefinite pronouns are plural; others can be singular or plural.)

CLOSE-UP   PRONOUN-ANTECEDENT AGREEMENT

In speech and in informal writing, many people use the plural pronouns *they* or *their* with singular indefinite pronouns that refer to people, such as *someone, everyone,* and *nobody.*

<u>Everyone</u> can present <u>their</u> own viewpoint.

In college writing, however, you should never use a plural pronoun with a singular subject. Instead, you can use both the masculine and the feminine pronoun.

<u>Everyone</u> can present <u>his or her</u> own viewpoint.

Or, you can make the sentence's subject plural.

<u>All participants</u> can present <u>their</u> own viewpoints.

The use of *his* alone to refer to a singular indefinite pronoun (Everyone can present *his* own viewpoint) is considered <u>**sexist language**</u>.

See 14d2

CHAPTER 6

USING VERBS CORRECTLY

6a Using Irregular Verbs

A **regular verb** forms both its past tense and its past participle by adding *-d* or *-ed* to the **base form** of the verb (the present tense form of the verb that is used with *I*).

PRINCIPAL PARTS OF REGULAR VERBS

Base Form	*Past Tense Form*	*Past Participle*
smile	smiled	smiled
talk	talked	talked

Irregular verbs do not follow this pattern. The chart that follows lists the principal parts of the most frequently used irregular verbs.

FREQUENTLY USED IRREGULAR VERBS

Base Form	*Past Tense Form*	*Past Participle*
arise	arose	arisen
awake	awoke, awaked	awoke, awaked
be	was/were	been
beat	beat	beaten
begin	began	begun
bend	bent	bent
bet	bet, betted	bet
bite	bit	bitten
blow	blew	blown
break	broke	broken
bring	brought	brought
build	built	built
burst	burst	burst
buy	bought	bought
catch	caught	caught
choose	chose	chosen
cling	clung	clung

continued on the following page

---

continued from the previous page

Base Form	Past Tense Form	Past Participle
come	came	come
cost	cost	cost
deal	dealt	dealt
dig	dug	dug
dive	dived, dove	dived
do	did	done
drag	dragged	dragged
draw	drew	drawn
drink	drank	drunk
drive	drove	driven
eat	ate	eaten
fall	fell	fallen
fight	fought	fought
find	found	found
fly	flew	flown
forget	forgot	forgotten, forgot
freeze	froze	frozen
get	got	gotten
give	gave	given
go	went	gone
grow	grew	grown
hang (suspend)	hung	hung
have	had	had
hear	heard	heard
keep	kept	kept
know	knew	known
lay	laid	laid
lead	led	led
lend	lent	lent
let	let	let
lie (recline)	lay	lain
make	made	made
prove	proved	proved, proven
read	read	read
ride	rode	ridden
ring	rang	rung
rise	rose	risen
run	ran	run
say	said	said
see	saw	seen
set (place)	set	set
shake	shook	shaken

continued on the following page

continued from the previous page

Base Form	Past Tense Form	Past Participle
shrink	shrank, shrunk	shrunk, shrunken
sing	sang	sung
sink	sank	sunk
sit	sat	sat
speak	spoke	spoken
speed	sped, speeded	sped, speeded
spin	spun	spun
spring	sprang	sprung
stand	stood	stood
steal	stole	stolen
strike	struck	struck, stricken
swear	swore	sworn
swim	swam	swum
swing	swung	swung
take	took	taken
teach	taught	taught
throw	threw	thrown
wake	woke, waked	waked, woken
wear	wore	worn
wring	wrung	wrung
write	wrote	written

CLOSE-UP

IRREGULAR VERBS: *LIE/LAY* AND *SIT/SET*

Lie means "to recline" and does not take an object ("He likes to *lie* on the floor"); *lay* means "to place" or "to put" and does take an object ("He wants to *lay* a rug on the floor"):

Base Form	Past Tense Form	Past Participle
lie	lay	lain
lay	laid	laid

Sit means "to assume a seated position" and does not take an object ("She wants to *sit* on the table"); set means "to place" or "to put" and usually takes an object ("She wants to *set* a vase on the table"):

Base Form	Past Tense Form	Past Participle
sit	sat	sat
set	set	set

6b Understanding Tense

Tense is the form a verb takes to indicate when an action occurred or when a condition existed.

ENGLISH VERB TENSES

Simple Tenses
Present (I *finish,* he or she *finishes*)
Past (I *finished*)
Future (I *will finish*)

Perfect Tenses
Present perfect (I *have finished,* he or she *has finished*)
Past perfect (I *had finished*)
Future perfect (I *will have finished*)

Progressive Tenses
Present progressive (I *am finishing,* he or she *is finishing*)
Past progressive (I *was finishing*)
Future progressive (I *will be finishing*)
Present perfect progressive (I *have been finishing*)
Past perfect progressive (I *had been finishing*)
Future perfect progressive (I *will have been finishing*)

---

(1) Using the Simple Tenses

The **simple tenses** include *present, past,* and *future.*

The **present tense** usually indicates an action that is taking place at the time it is expressed in speech or writing or an action that occurs regularly.

I <u>see</u> your point. (an action taking place when it is expressed)

We <u>wear</u> wool in the winter. (an action that occurs regularly)

SPECIAL USES OF THE PRESENT TENSE

The present tense has four special uses.

TO INDICATE FUTURE TIME: The grades <u>arrive</u> next Thursday.

TO STATE A GENERALLY HELD BELIEF: Studying <u>pays</u> off.

continued on the following page

continued from the previous page

TO STATE A SCIENTIFIC TRUTH: An object at rest <u>tends</u> to stay at rest.

TO DISCUSS A LITERARY WORK: *Family Installments* <u>tells</u> the story of a Puerto Rican family.

The **past tense** indicates that an action has already taken place.

John Glenn <u>orbited</u> the Earth three times on February 20, 1962. (an action completed in the past)

As a young man, Mark Twain <u>traveled</u> through the Southwest. (an action that occurred once or many times in the past but did not extend into the present)

The **future tense** indicates that an action will or is likely to take place.

Halley's Comet <u>will reappear</u> in 2061. (a future action that will definitely occur)

The land boom in Nevada <u>will</u> probably <u>continue</u>. (a future action that is likely to occur)

(2) Using the Perfect Tenses

The **perfect tenses** designate actions that were or will be completed before other actions or conditions. The perfect tenses are formed with the appropriate tense form of the auxiliary verb *have* plus the past participle.

The **present perfect** tense can indicate two types of continuing action beginning in the past.

Dr. Kim <u>has finished</u> studying the effects of BHA on rats. (an action that began in the past and is finished at the present time)

My mother <u>has invested</u> her money wisely. (an action that began in the past and extends into the present)

The **past perfect** tense indicates an action occurring before a certain time in the past.

By 1946, engineers <u>had built</u> the first electronic digital computer.

The **future perfect** tense indicates that an action will be finished by a certain future time.

By Tuesday, the transit authority <u>will have run</u> out of money.

(3) Using the Progressive Tenses

The **progressive tenses** express continuing action. They are formed with the appropriate tense of the verb *be* plus the present participle.

The **present progressive** tense indicates that something is happening at the time it is expressed in speech or writing.

The volcano <u>is erupting</u>, and lava <u>is flowing</u> toward the town.

The **past progressive** tense indicates two kinds of past action.

Roderick Usher's actions <u>were becoming</u> increasingly bizarre. (a continuing action in the past)

The French revolutionary Marat was stabbed to death while he <u>was bathing</u>. (an action occurring at the same time in the past as another action)

The **future progressive** tense indicates a continuing action in the future.

The treasury secretary <u>will be monitoring</u> the money supply very carefully.

The **present perfect progressive** tense indicates action continuing from the past into the present and possibly into the future.

Rescuers <u>have been working</u> around the clock.

The **past perfect progressive** tense indicates that a past action went on until another one occurred.

Before President Kennedy was assassinated, he <u>had been working</u> on civil rights legislation.

The **future perfect progressive** tense indicates that an action will continue until a certain future time.

By eleven o'clock we <u>will have been driving</u> for seven hours.

6c Understanding Mood

Mood is the form a verb takes to indicate whether a writer is making a statement, asking a question, giving a command, or expressing a wish or a contrary-to-fact statement. There are three moods in English: the *indicative,* the *imperative,* and the *subjunctive.*

The **indicative** mood states a fact, expresses an opinion, or asks a question: Jackie Robinson <u>had</u> a great impact on professional baseball.

The **imperative** mood is used in commands and direct requests: <u>Use</u> a dictionary.

The **subjunctive** mood causes the greatest difficulty for writers.

The **present subjunctive** uses the base form of the verb, regardless of the subject.

Dr. Gorman suggested that he <u>study</u> the Cambrian period.

The present subjunctive is used in *that* clauses after words such as *ask, suggest, require, recommend,* and *demand.*

The report recommended that doctors <u>be</u> more flexible.

Captain Ahab insisted that his crew <u>hunt</u> the white whale.

The **past subjunctive** has the same form as the past tense of the verb.

He wished he <u>had</u> more time.

The past subjunctive is used in **conditional statements** (statements beginning with *if, as if,* or *as though* that are contrary to fact and statements that express a wish).

If John <u>went</u> home, he could see Marsha. (John is not home.)

The father acted as if he <u>were</u> having the baby. (The father couldn't be having the baby.)

I wish I <u>were</u> more organized. (expresses a wish)

NOTE: In the past subjunctive, the verb *be* takes the form *were* (not *was*) even with a singular subject.

6d   Understanding Voice

Voice is the form a verb takes to indicate whether its subject acts or is acted upon. When the subject of a verb does something—that is, acts—the verb is in the **active voice.** When the subject of a verb receives the action—that is, is acted upon—the verb is in the **passive voice.**

ACTIVE VOICE: Hart Crane <u>wrote</u> *The Bridge.*

PASSIVE VOICE: *The Bridge* <u>was written</u> by Hart Crane.

NOTE: Because the active voice emphasizes the doer of an action, it is usually clearer and more emphatic than the passive voice. Whenever possible, use active voice in your college writing.

CHAPTER 7

USING PRONOUNS CORRECTLY

7a **Understanding Pronoun Case**

Pronouns change **case** to indicate their function in a sentence. English has three cases: *subjective, objective,* and *possessive.*

PRONOUN CASE FORMS

Subjective

I	he, she	it	we	you	they	who	whoever

Objective

me	him, her	it	us	you	them	whom	whomever

Possessive

my	his, her	its	our	your	their	whose
mine	hers		ours	yours	theirs	

---

(1) Subjective Case

A pronoun takes the **subjective case** in the following situations.

SUBJECT OF A VERB: <u>I</u> bought a new mountain bike.

SUBJECT COMPLEMENT: It was <u>he</u> for whom the men were looking.

(2) Objective Case

A pronoun takes the **objective case** in these situations.

DIRECT OBJECT: Our sociology teacher asked Adam and <u>me</u> to work on the project.

INDIRECT OBJECT: The plumber's bill gave <u>him</u> quite a shock.

OBJECT OF A PREPOSITION: Between <u>us</u> we own ten shares of stock.

PRONOUN CASE IN COMPOUND CONSTRUCTIONS

I is not necessarily more appropriate than *me*. In compound constructions like the following, *me* is correct.

Just between you and <u>me</u> [not *I*], I think the data are incomplete. (*Me* is the object of the preposition *between*.)

(3) Possessive Case

A pronoun takes the **possessive case** when it indicates ownership (*our* car, *your* book). The possessive case is also used before a <u>gerund</u>.

See A1.3

Napoleon approved of <u>their</u> [not *them*] ruling Naples. (*Ruling* is a gerund.)

7b Determining Pronoun Case in Special Situations

(1) Comparisons with *Than* or *As*

When a comparison ends with a pronoun, the pronoun's function in the sentence dictates your choice of pronoun case. If the pronoun functions as a subject, use the subjective case; if it functions as an object, use the objective case.

Darcy likes John more than <u>I</u>. (*I* is the subject: more than *I* like John)

Darcy likes John more than <u>me</u>. (*me* is the object: more than she likes *me*)

(2) *Who* and *Whom*

The case of the pronouns *who* and *whom* depends on their function *within their own clause*. When a pronoun serves as the subject of its clause, use *who* or *whoever*; when it functions as an object, use *whom* or *whomever*.

The Salvation Army gives food and shelter to <u>whoever</u> is in need. (*Whoever* is the subject of a dependent clause.)

I wonder <u>whom</u> jazz musician Miles Davis influenced. (*Whom* is the object of *influenced* in the dependent clause.)

PRONOUN CASE IN QUESTIONS

To determine the case of *who* at the beginning of a question, use a personal pronoun to answer the question. The case of *who* should be the same as the case of the personal pronoun.

<u>Who</u> wrote *The Age of Innocence?* (<u>She</u> wrote it— subject)

<u>Whom</u> do you support for mayor? (I support <u>her</u>— object)

---

(3) Appositives

An **appositive** is a noun or noun phrase that identifies or re-names an adjacent noun or pronoun. The case of a pronoun in an appositive depends on the function of the word the appositive identifies.

We heard two Motown recording artists, Smokey Robinson and <u>him</u>. (*Artists* is the object of the verb *heard,* so the pronoun in the appositive *Smokey Robinson and him* takes the objective case.)

Two Motown recording artists, Smokey Robinson and <u>he</u>, recorded for Motown Records. (*Artists* is the subject of the sentence, so the pronoun in the appositive *Smokey Robinson and he* takes the subjective case.)

(4) *We* and *Us* Before a Noun

When a first-person plural pronoun precedes a noun, the case of the pronoun depends on the way the noun functions in the sentence.

<u>We</u> women must stick together. (*Women* is the subject of the sentence, so the pronoun *we* must be in the subjective case.)

Teachers make learning easy for <u>us</u> students. (*Students* is the object of the preposition *for,* so the pronoun *us* must be in the objective case.)

7c Revising Common Errors of Pronoun Reference

An **antecedent** is the word or word group to which a pronoun refers. The connection between a pronoun and its antecedent should always be clear.

(1) Ambiguous Antecedents

Sometimes a pronoun—for example, *this, that, which,* or *it*—appears to refer to more than one antecedent. In such cases, substitute a noun for the pronoun.

The accountant took out his calculator and completed the
tax return. Then, he put ~~it~~ the calculator into his briefcase.

Sometimes a pronoun does not seem to refer to any specific antecedent. In such cases, supply a noun to clarify the reference.

Some one-celled organisms contain chlorophyll yet are considered animals. This paradox illustrates the difficulty of classifying single-celled organisms.

(2) Remote Antecedents

The farther a pronoun is from its antecedent, the more difficult it is for readers to make a connection between them. If a pronoun's antecedent is far away from it, replace the pronoun with a noun.

During the mid-1800s, many Czechs began to immigrate to America. By 1860, about 23,000 Czechs had left their country. By 1900, 13,000 Czech immigrants were coming to ~~its~~ America's shores each year.

(3) Nonexistent Antecedents

Sometimes a pronoun refers to a nonexistent antecedent. In such cases, replace the pronoun with a noun.

Our township has decided to build a computer lab in the elementary school. ~~They~~ Teachers feel that fourth-graders should begin using computers.

WHO, WHICH, AND THAT

In general, *who* refers to people or to animals that have names. *Which* and *that* refer to objects, events, or unnamed animals. When referring to an antecedent, be sure to choose the appropriate pronoun (*who, which,* or *that*).

David Henry Hwang, <u>who</u> wrote the Tony Award-winning play *M. Butterfly,* also wrote *Family Devotions* and *FOB.*

The spotted owl, <u>which</u> lives in old-growth forests, is in danger of extinction.

Houses <u>that</u> are built today are usually more energy efficient than those built twenty years ago.

CHAPTER 8

USING ADJECTIVES AND ADVERBS CORRECTLY

Adjectives modify nouns and pronouns. **Adverbs** modify verbs, adjectives, or other adverbs—or entire phrases, clauses, or sentences.

The *function* of a word, not its *form*, determines whether it is an adjective or an adverb. Although many adverbs (such as *immediately* and *hopelessly*) end in *-ly*, others (such as *almost* and *very*) do not. Moreover, some words that end in *-ly* (such as *lively*) are adjectives.

8a Using Adjectives as Subject Complements

See A1.3

Be sure to use an adjective, not an adverb, as a subject complement. A <u>subject complement</u> is a word that follows a linking verb and modifies the sentence's subject, not its verb. A **linking verb** does not show physical or emotional action. *Seem, appear, believe, become, grow, turn, remain, prove, look, sound, smell, taste, feel,* and the forms of the verb *be* are or can be used as linking verbs.

> Michelle seemed <u>brave</u>. (*Seemed* shows no action and is therefore a linking verb. Because *brave* is a subject complement that modifies the noun *Michelle*, it takes the adjective form.)

> Michelle smiled <u>bravely</u>. (*Smiled* shows action, so it is not a linking verb. *Bravely* modifies *smiled*, so it takes the adverb form.)

NOTE: Sometimes the same verb can function as either a linking verb or an action verb.

> He looked <u>hungry</u>. (*Looked* is a linking verb; *hungry* modifies the subject.)

> He looked <u>hungrily</u> at the sandwich. (*Looked* is an action verb; *hungrily* modifies the verb.)

8b Using Adverbs Appropriately

Be sure to use an adverb, not an adjective, to modify verbs, adjectives, or other adverbs—or entire phrases, clauses, or sentences.

Most students did ~~great~~ very well on the midterm.

My parents dress a lot more conservative‸ly than my friends do.

 USING ADJECTIVES AND ADVERBS

In informal speech, adjective forms such as *good, bad, sure, real, slow, quick,* and *loud* are often used to modify verbs, adjectives, and adverbs. Avoid these informal modifiers in college writing.

The program ran ~~real good~~ really well the first time we tried it, but the new system performed ~~bad~~ badly.

 Using Comparative and Superlative Forms

COMPARATIVE AND SUPERLATIVE FORMS

Form	Function	Example
Positive	Describes a quality; indicates no comparisons	big
Comparative	Indicates comparisons between *two* qualities (greater or lesser)	bigger
Superlative	Indicates comparisons among *more than two* qualities (greatest or least)	biggest

NOTE: Some adverbs, particularly those indicating time, place, and degree (*almost, very, here, yesterday,* and *immediately*), do not have comparative or superlative forms.

---

(1) Regular Comparatives and Superlatives

To form the comparative and superlative, all one-syllable adjectives and many two-syllable adjectives (particularly those that end in *-y, -ly, -le, -er,* and *-ow*) add *-er* or *-est:* slow<u>er</u>, funni<u>er</u>; slow<u>est</u>, funni<u>est</u>. (Note that a final *y* becomes *i* before the *-er* or *-est* is added.)

Other two-syllable adjectives and all long adjectives form the comparative with *more* and the superlative with *most:* <u>more</u> famous, <u>more</u> incredible; <u>most</u> famous, <u>most</u> incredible.

Adverbs ending in *-ly* also form the comparative with *more* and the superlative with *most:* <u>more</u> slowly; <u>most</u> slowly. Other adverbs use the *-er* and *-est* endings: soon<u>er</u>; soon<u>est</u>.

All adjectives and adverbs indicate a lesser degree with *less* (<u>less</u> lovely; <u>less</u> slowly) and the least degree with *least* (<u>least</u> lovely; <u>least</u> slowly).

USING COMPARATIVES AND SUPERLATIVES

Never use both *more* and *-er* to form the comparative, and never use both *most* and *-est* to form the superlative.

Nothing could have been ~~more~~ easier.

Jack is the ~~most~~ meanest person in town.

Never use the superlative when comparing only two things.

Stacy is the ~~oldest~~ older of the two sisters.

Never use the comparative when comparing more than two things.

We chose the ~~earlier~~ earliest of the four appointments.

(2) Irregular Comparatives and Superlatives

Some adjectives and adverbs have irregular comparative and superlative forms.

IRREGULAR COMPARATIVES AND SUPERLATIVES

	Positive	*Comparative*	*Superlative*
Adjectives:	good	better	best
	bad	worse	worst
	a little	less	least
	many, some, much	more	most
Adverbs:	well	better	best
	badly	worse	worst

ILLOGICAL COMPARISONS

Many adjectives and adverbs can logically exist only in the positive degree. For example, words such as *perfect, unique, empty, excellent, impossible, parallel,* and *dead* cannot have comparative or superlative forms.

I read ~~the most~~ ^{an} excellent story.

The vase in her collection was ~~very~~ unique.

PART 3

WRITING EFFECTIVE SENTENCES

CHAPTER 9

WRITING VARIED SENTENCES

9a Using Compound and Complex Sentences

Paragraphs that mix **simple sentences** with compound and complex sentences are more varied—and therefore more interesting—than those that do not. See A2.2

(1) Compound Sentences

A **compound sentence** is created when two or more independent clauses are joined with *coordinating conjunctions, transitional words and phrases, correlative conjunctions, semicolons,* or *colons.*

Coordinating Conjunctions
The pianist made some mistakes, <u>but</u> the concert was a success.

NOTE: Use a comma before a coordinating conjunction—*and, or, nor, but, for, so,* and *yet*—that joins two **independent clauses**. See A1.7

Transitional Words and Phrases
The saxophone does not belong to the brass family; <u>in fact,</u> it is a member of the woodwind family.

Correlative Conjunctions
<u>Either</u> he left his coat in his locker, <u>or</u> he left it on the bus.

Semicolons
Alaska is the largest state; Rhode Island is the smallest.

Colons
He got his orders: he was to leave for France on Sunday.

NOTE: Use a semicolon—not a comma—before a transitional word or phrase that joins two independent clauses. Frequently used **transitional words and phrases** include conjunctive adverbs like *consequently, finally, still,* and *thus* as well as expressions like *for example, in fact,* and *for instance.* See 2b

(2) Complex Sentences

A **complex sentence** consists of one independent clause and at least one **dependent clause**. A **subordinating conjunction** or **relative pronoun** links the independent and dependent clauses and indicates the relationship between them. See A1.7

(dependent clause)   (independent clause)
[After the town was evacuated], [the hurricane began].

(independent clause)   (dependent clause)
[Officials watched the storm], [which threatened to destroy the town].

(dependent clause)
Town officials, [who were very concerned], watched the storm.

FREQUENTLY USED SUBORDINATING CONJUNCTIONS

after	before	until
although	if	when
as	once	whenever
as if	since	where
as though	that	wherever
because	unless	while

RELATIVE PRONOUNS

that	whatever	who (whose, whom)
what	which	whoever (whomever)

9b Varying Sentence Length

Strings of short simple sentences can be tedious—and sometimes hard to follow, as the following paragraph indicates.

> John Peter Zenger was a newspaper editor. He waged and won an important battle for freedom of the press in America. He criticized the policies of the British governor. He was charged with criminal libel as a result. Zenger's lawyers were disbarred by the governor. Andrew Hamilton defended him. Hamilton convinced the jury that Zenger's criticisms were true. Therefore, the statements were not libelous.

You can revise choppy sentences like these by using *coordination, subordination,* or *embedding* to combine them with adjacent sentences.

Coordination pairs similar elements—words, phrases, or clauses—giving equal weight to each.

Two choppy sentences linked with *and,* creating compound sentence

> John Peter Zenger was a newspaper editor. He waged and won an important battle for freedom of the press in America. He criticized the policies of the British governor, and he was charged with criminal libel as a result. Zenger's lawyers were disbarred by the governor. Andrew Hamilton defended him. Hamilton convinced the jury that Zenger's criticisms were true. Therefore, the statements were not libelous.

Subordination places the more important idea in an independent clause and the less important idea in a dependent clause.

John Peter Zenger was a newspaper editor who waged and won an important battle for freedom of the press in America. He criticized the policies of the British governor, and he was charged with criminal libel as a result. When Zenger's lawyers were disbarred by the governor, Andrew Hamilton defended him. Hamilton convinced the jury that Zenger's criticisms were true. Therefore, the statements were not libelous.

Simple sentences become dependent clauses, creating two complex sentences

Embedding is the working of additional words and phrases into sentences.

John Peter Zenger was a newspaper editor who waged and won an important battle for freedom of the press in America. He criticized the policies of the British governor, and he was charged with criminal libel as a result. When Zenger's lawyers were disbarred by the governor, Andrew Hamilton defended him, convincing the jury that Zenger's criticisms were true. Therefore, the statements were not libelous.

The sentence Hamilton convinced the jury . . . *becomes the phrase* convincing the jury

This final revision of the original string of choppy sentences uses coordination, subordination, and embedding to vary sentence length, retaining the final short simple sentence for emphasis.

9c Varying Sentence Types

Another way to achieve sentence variety is to mix **declarative** sentences (statements) with occasional **imperative** sentences (commands or requests), **exclamatory** sentences, and **rhetorical questions** (questions that the reader is not expected to answer).

See A2.2

Local television newscasts seem to be delivering less and less news. Although we tune in to be updated on local, national, and world events, only about 30 percent of most newscasts is devoted to news. The remaining time is spent on feature stories, advertising, weather, sports, and casual conversation between anchors. Given this focus on "soft" material, what options do those of us wishing to find out what happened in the world have? [**rhetorical question**] Critics of local television have a few suggestions. First, write to your local station's management voicing your concern; then, try to get others to sign a petition. [**imperatives**] If changes are not made, you can turn off your television. Better yet, read the newspaper! [**exclamation**]

9d Varying Sentence Openings

Rather than beginning every sentence with the subject, begin with modifying words, phrases, or clauses.

Words
<u>Proud</u> and <u>relieved</u>, they watched their daughter receive her diploma. (adjectives)

Phrases
<u>For better or worse</u>, credit cards are now widely available to college students. (prepositional phrase)

<u>Located on the west coast of Great Britain</u>, Wales is part of the United Kingdom. (participial phrase)

<u>His interests widening</u>, Picasso designed ballet sets and illustrated books. (absolute phrase)

Clauses
<u>After Woodrow Wilson was incapacitated by a stroke</u>, his wife unofficially performed many presidential duties. (adverb clause)

9e Varying Standard Word Order

(1) Inverting Word Order
You can vary standard subject-verb-object (or complement) word order by placing the complement or direct object *before* the verb instead of in its conventional position or by placing the verb *before* the subject instead of after it.

> (object) (verb)
> A cheery smile he had for everyone.
>   (subject)

> (complement)
> Hardest hit were the coastal areas.
>   (verb)   (subject)

Inverting word order draws attention to the word or word group that appears in an unexpected place—but inverted word order can be distracting, so use it in moderation.

(2) Separating Subject From Verb
You can also vary conventional word order by placing words or phrases between the subject and verb—but be sure that the word group does not obscure the connection between subject and verb or create an **agreement** error.

See 5a1

> (subject)   (verb)
> Many <u>states</u>, hoping to reduce needless fatalities, <u>require</u> that children ride in government-approved child safety seats.

CHAPTER 10

WRITING CONCISE SENTENCES

A sentence is not concise simply because it is short; a concise sentence contains only the words necessary to make its point.

10a Eliminating Nonessential Words

Whenever possible, delete nonessential words—*deadwood, utility words,* and *circumlocution*—from your writing.

(1) Eliminating Deadwood
Deadwood is a term used for unnecessary phrases that simply take up space and add nothing to meaning.

~~There were~~ Many factors ~~that~~ influenced his decision to become a priest.

Shoppers ~~who are~~ looking for bargains often go to outlets.

They played ~~a~~ an exhausting racquetball game ~~that was exhausting~~.

~~In this~~ This article ~~it~~ discusses lead poisoning.

Deadwood also includes unnecessary statements of opinion, such as *I feel, it seems to me,* and *in my opinion.*

~~In my opinion, I believe the~~ The characters seem undeveloped.

~~As far as I'm concerned, this~~ This course looks interesting.

(2) Eliminating Utility Words
Utility words are fillers; they contribute nothing to a sentence. Utility words include nouns with imprecise meanings (*factor, situation, type, aspect,* and so on); adjectives so general that they are almost meaningless (*good, bad, important*); and common adverbs denoting degree (*basically, actually, quite, very, definitely*). Often you can just delete a utility word; if you cannot, replace it with a more precise word.

~~The registration situation~~ Registration was disorganized.

53

The scholarship ~~basically~~ offered Fran ~~a good~~ ^{an} opportunity to study Spanish.

It was ~~actually~~ a worthwhile book, but I didn't ~~completely~~ finish it.

(3) Eliminating Circumlocution

Taking a roundabout way to say something (using ten words when five will do) is called **circumlocution.** Instead of complicated constructions, use concise, specific words and phrases that come right to the point.

^{The}
~~It is not unlikely that the~~ trend toward lower consumer
spending will continue.
^{probably}

Joel was in the army ~~during the same time that~~ ^{while} I was in college.

REVISING WORDY PHRASES

If you cannot edit a wordy construction, substitute a more concise, more direct term.

Wordy	Concise
at the present time	now
due to the fact that	because
in the vicinity of	near
have the ability to	be able to

10b Eliminating Unnecessary Repetition

Unnecessary repetition and redundant word groups (repeated words or phrases that say the same thing) can annoy readers and obscure your meaning. Correct unnecessary repetition by using one of the following strategies.

(1) Deleting Redundancy

People's clothing ~~attire~~ can reveal a good deal about their personalities.

(2) Substituting a Pronoun

Fictional detective Miss Marple has solved many crimes. *The Murder at the Vicarage* was one of ~~Miss Marple's~~ ^{her} most challenging cases.

(3) Creating an Appositive

Red Barber, ~~was~~ a sportscaster, ~~He~~ was known for his colorful expressions.

(4) Creating a Compound

John F. Kennedy was the youngest man ever elected president, *and* ~~He was~~ also the first Catholic to hold this office.

(5) Creating a Complex Sentence

Americans value freedom of speech, *which* ~~Freedom of speech~~ is guaranteed by the First Amendment.

10c Tightening Rambling Sentences

The combination of nonessential words, unnecessary repetition, and complicated syntax creates **rambling sentences.** Revising rambling sentences frequently requires extensive editing.

(1) Eliminating Excessive Coordination

When you string a series of clauses together with coordinating conjunctions, you create a rambling, unfocused **compound sentence**. To revise such sentences, first identify the main idea or ideas, and then subordinate the supporting details.

See 9a1

Benjamin Franklin, ~~was~~ the son of a candlemaker, ~~but he~~ later apprenticed with his half-brother as a printer, *an* ~~and this~~ experience *that* led to his buying *The Pennsylvania Gazette,* *which* ~~and~~ he managed ~~this periodical~~ with great success.

(2) Eliminating Adjective Clauses

A series of **adjective clauses** is also likely to produce a rambling sentence. To revise, substitute concise modifying words or phrases for adjective clauses.

See A2.3

Moby-Dick, ~~which is~~ a novel about a white whale, was written by Herman Melville, who *revised the first draft at the urging of his* ~~was~~ friend~~ly with~~ Nathaniel Hawthorne, ~~who urged him to revise the first draft.~~

(3) Eliminating Passive Constructions

See 6d
Excessive use of the **passive voice** can create rambling sentences. Correct this problem by changing passive voice to active voice.

Concerned Americans are organizing

∧ "Buy American" rallies, ~~are being organized by concerned~~
            hoping ∧
~~Americans who hope~~ that ~~jobs can be saved by~~ such gatherings, can save jobs.

(4) Eliminating Wordy Prepositional Phrases

See A2.3
When you revise, substitute adjectives or adverbs for wordy **prepositional phrases**.

          dangerous   exciting
The trip was ~~one of danger~~ but also ~~one of excitement~~.
          confidently   authoritatively
He spoke ~~in a confident manner~~ and ~~with a lot of authority~~.

(5) Eliminating Wordy Noun Constructions

See A2.3
Substitute strong verbs for wordy **noun phrases**.

         decided
We have ~~made the decision~~ to postpone the meeting until ~~the~~
~~appearance of~~ all the board members. appear
                                ∧

CHAPTER 11

REVISING AWKWARD
OR CONFUSING SENTENCES

The most common causes of awkward or confusing sentences are *unwarranted shifts, mixed constructions, faulty predication,* and *illogical comparisons.*

11a Revising Unwarranted Shifts

(1) Shifts in Tense

Verb **tense** in a sentence or in a related group of sentences should not shift without good reason—to indicate changes of time, for example. See 6b

The Wizard of Oz <u>is</u> a classic film that <u>was made</u> in 1939. (acceptable shift from present to past)

Unwarranted shifts in tense can be confusing.

I registered for the advanced philosophy seminar because I wanted a challenge. However, by the first week I ~~start~~ started having trouble understanding the reading.

Jack Kerouac's novel *On the Road* follows a group of friends who ~~drove~~ drive across the United States in the 1950s.

(2) Shifts in Voice

Unwarranted shifts from active to passive **voice** (or from passive to active) can be confusing. In the following sentence, for instance, the shift from active (*wrote*) to passive (*was written*) makes it unclear who wrote *The Great Gatsby.* See 6d

F. Scott Fitzgerald wrote *This Side of Paradise,* and later *The Great Gatsby.* ~~was written.~~ wrote

NOTE: Sometimes a shift from active to passive voice within a sentence may be necessary to give the sentence proper emphasis.

> Even though consumers <u>protested</u>, the sales tax <u>was increased</u>. (To say *the legislature increased the sales tax* would draw the emphasis away from *consumers*.)

(3) Shifts in Mood

^{See}
^{6c}
     Unnecessary shifts in **<u>mood</u>** can also create awkward sentences.

> Next, heat the mixture in a test tube, and ~~you should make~~ ^{be} sure it does not boil. (shift from imperative to indicative)

(4) Shifts in Person and Number

Person indicates who is speaking (first person—*I, we*), who is spoken to (second person—*you*), and who is spoken about (third person—*he, she, it,* and *they*). Unwarranted shifts between the second and the third person are most often responsible for awkward sentences.

> When ~~someone~~ ^{you} look**s** for a car loan, you compare the interest rates of several banks. (shift from third to second person)

Number indicates one (singular—*novel, it*) or more than one (plural—*novels, they, them*). Unwarranted shifts in number can create awkward sentences, so be sure singular pronouns refer to
^{See}
^{5b}
singular **<u>antecedents</u>** and plural pronouns to plural antecedents.

> If a person does not study regularly, ~~they~~ ^{he or she} will have a difficult time passing Spanish. (shift from singular to plural)

11b   Revising Mixed Constructions

A **mixed construction** is created when a dependent clause, prepositional phrase, or independent clause is incorrectly used as the subject of a sentence.

> Because she studies every day, ~~explains why~~ she gets good grades. (dependent clause used as subject)

> By calling for information, ~~is the way to~~ ^{you can} learn more about the benefits of ROTC. (prepositional phrase used as subject)

Faulty Predication   **awkward 11c**

Being
~~He was~~ late ~~was what~~ made him miss Act 1. (independent
clause used as subject)

11c Revising Faulty Predication

Faulty predication occurs when a sentence's predicate does
not logically complete its subject. Faulty predication is especially common in sentences that contain a linking verb—a form
of the verb *be*, for example—and a subject complement.

caused
Mounting costs and decreasing revenues ~~were~~ the downfall
of the hospital.

Faulty predication also occurs in sentences that contain a
construction like *is where* or *is when*. *Is* must be preceded and
followed by a noun or noun phrase.

the construction of
Taxidermy is ~~where you construct~~ a lifelike representation of
an animal from its preserved skin.

Faulty predication also occurs when the phrase *the reason
is* precedes *because*. In this situation, *because* (which means "for
the reason that") is redundant and can be deleted.

that
The reason we drive is ~~because~~ we are afraid to fly.

CHAPTER 12

USING PARALLELISM

Parallelism—the use of matching words, phrases, clauses, or sentence structures to express equivalent ideas—adds unity, balance, and force to your writing. Remember, however, that although effective parallelism can help you write clearer sentences, faulty parallelism can create awkward sentences that obscure your meaning and confuse readers.

12a Using Parallelism Effectively

(1) With Items in a Series

Eat, drink, and be merry.

Baby food consumption, toy production, and marijuana use are likely to decline as the U.S. population ages.

(2) With Paired Items

Paired words, phrases, or clauses should be presented in parallel terms.

The thank-you note was short but sweet.

Ask not what your country can do for you; ask what you can do for your country. (John F. Kennedy, *inaugural address*)

Paired items linked by **correlative conjunctions** (such as *not only . . . but also* and *either . . . or*) should always be parallel.

The designer paid attention not only to color but also to texture.

Either repeat physics or take calculus.

Parallelism is also used with paired elements linked by *than* or *as*.

Richard Wright and James Baldwin chose to live in Paris rather than to remain in the United States.

See
27e1, **NOTE:** Elements in **lists** and **outlines** should also be parallel.
34b

60

12b Revising Faulty Parallelism

Faulty parallelism occurs when elements that have the same function in a sentence are not presented in parallel terms.

Many developing countries lack sufficient housing, sufficient
food, and ~~their~~ health-care facilities ~~are also insufficient.~~
(*sufficient*)

To correct faulty parallelism, match nouns with nouns, verbs with verbs, and phrases or clauses with similarly constructed phrases or clauses.

Popular exercises for men and women include spinning,
weight ~~lifters~~, and jogging.
(*lifting*)

I look forward to hearing from you and to ~~have~~ an opportunity
(*having*)
to tell you more about myself.

REPEATING KEY WORDS

Although the use of similar grammatical structures may be enough to convey parallelism, sometimes sentences are even clearer if certain key words (for example, prepositions that introduce items in a series) are also parallel. In the following sentence, repeating the preposition *by* makes it clear that *not* applies only to the first phase.

Computerization has helped industry by not allowing
labor costs to skyrocket, ∧ increasing the speed of pro-
(*by*)
duction, and ∧ improving efficiency.
(*by*)

CHAPTER 13

PLACING MODIFIERS CAREFULLY

A **modifier** is a word, phrase, or clause that describes, limits, or qualifies another word or word group in the sentence. A modifier should be placed close to its **headword,** the word or phrase it modifies. **Faulty modification** is the confusing placement of modifiers or the modification of nonexistent words.

13a Revising Misplaced Modifiers

A **misplaced modifier** is a word or word group whose placement suggests that it modifies one word or phrase when it is intended to modify another.

Λ ~~Dark~~ and threatening. ~~Wendy watched the storm~~. (Was Wendy watched the storm, dark

Wendy dark and threatening?)

(1) Placing Modifying Words Precisely
Limiting modifiers such as *almost, only, even,* and *just* should immediately precede the words they modify. A different placement will change the meaning of a sentence.

Nick *just* set up camp at the edge of town. (He did it just now.)

Just Nick set up camp at the edge of town. (He did it alone.)

Nick set up camp *just* at the edge of town. (His camp was precisely at the edge.)

When a limiting modifier is placed so that it is not clear whether it modifies a word before it or one after it, it is called a *squinting modifier.*

The life that everyone thought would fulfill her <u>totally</u> bored her.

To correct a squinting modifier, place the modifier so that it clearly modifies its headword.

The life that everyone thought would <u>totally</u> fulfill her bored her. (She was expected to be totally fulfilled.)

The life that everyone thought would fulfill her bored her <u>totally</u>. (She was totally bored.)

(2) Relocating Misplaced Phrases

When you revise, relocate misplaced verbal phrases, placing them directly before or directly after the words or word groups they modify.

Roller-skating along the shore,
∧ Jane watched the boats. ~~roller-skating along the shore.~~

Place prepositional phrase modifiers immediately after the words they modify.

with no arms
Venus de Milo is a statue ∧ created by a famous artist ~~with no arms~~.

(3) Relocating Misplaced Dependent Clauses

An adjective clause usually appears immediately after the word it modifies.

, which will benefit everyone,
This diet program ∧ will limit the consumption of possible carcinogens ~~which will benefit everyone~~.

An adverb clause may appear in various positions, but its relationship to its headword must be clear and logical.

After they had a glass of wine, the
~~The~~ parents checked to see that the children were sleeping. ~~after they had a glass of wine.~~

13b Revising Intrusive Modifiers

An **intrusive modifier** interrupts a sentence, making the sentence difficult to understand.

Revise when a long modifying phrase comes between an auxiliary verb and a main verb.

Without
~~She had, without~~ giving it a second thought or considering
she had
the consequences, planned to reenlist.
∧

Revise when modifiers awkwardly interrupt an **infinitive**, coming between the word *to* and the base form of the verb.

See
A1.3

defeat his opponent
He hoped to ∧ quickly and easily. ~~defeat his opponent~~.

13c Revising Dangling Modifiers

A **dangling modifier** is a word or phrase that cannot logically modify any word or word group in the sentence.

Using this drug, many undesirable side effects are experienced.

One way to correct this dangling modifier is to create a new subject by adding a word or word group that *using this drug* can modify.

Using this drug, <u>patients</u> experience many undesirable side effects.

Another way to correct the dangling modifier is to change it into a dependent clause.

Many undesirable side effects are experienced <u>when this drug is used</u>.

DANGLING MODIFIERS AND THE PASSIVE VOICE

See 6d

Most sentences that include dangling modifiers do not include a headword because they are in the passive voice. Changing the **passive voice** to the **active voice** corrects the dangling modifier by changing the subject of the sentence's main clause (*side effects*) to a word that the dangling modifier can logically modify (*patients*).

CHAPTER 14

CHOOSING THE RIGHT WORD

14a Avoiding Jargon

Jargon, the specialized or technical vocabulary of a trade, profession, or academic discipline, is useful for communicating in the field for which it was developed, but outside that field it can be confusing.

The patient had a~~n acute myocardial infarction~~ a heart attack.

When you write, use vocabulary that is appropriate for your audience and purpose.

14b Avoiding Pretentious Diction

Good writing is clear writing, and pompous or flowery language is no substitute for clarity. Revise to eliminate **pretentious diction,** inappropriately elevated and wordy language.

As I fell ~~into slumber~~ asleep, I ~~cogitated~~ thought about my day ~~ambling~~ hiking through ~~the splendor of~~ the Appalachian Mountains.

14c Avoiding Clichés

Clichés are trite expressions that have lost all meaning because they have been so overused. Familiar sayings like "happy as a clam," and "what goes around comes around," for example, do little to enhance your writing. Avoid the temptation to use clichés in your college writing. Take the time to think of fresh language.

14d Avoiding Biased Language

(1) Offensive Labels

When referring to a racial, ethnic, or religious group, use words with neutral connotations or words that the group itself uses in *formal* speech or writing. Also avoid potentially offensive labels related to age, class, occupation, physical ability, or sexual orientation.

(2) Sexist Language

Sexist language entails much more than the use of derogatory words such as *hunk* and *bimbo*. Assuming that some professions are exclusive to one gender—for instance, that *nurse* denotes only women or that *engineer* denotes only men—is also sexist. So is the use of job titles such as *postman* for *letter carrier* and *stewardess* for *flight attendant*.

Sexist language also occurs when a writer fails to apply the same terminology to both men and women. For example, you should refer to two scientists with Ph.D.s not as Dr. Sagan and Mrs. Yallow, but as Dr. Sagan and Dr. Yallow.

In your writing, always use *women*—not *girls* or *ladies*—when referring to adult females. Also avoid using the generic *he* or *him* when your subject could be either male or female. Instead, use the third-person plural or the phrase *he or she* (not *he/she*).

SEXIST: Before boarding, each <u>passenger</u> should make certain that <u>he</u> has <u>his</u> ticket.

REVISED: Before boarding, <u>passengers</u> should make certain that <u>they</u> have <u>their</u> tickets.

REVISED: Before boarding, each <u>passenger</u> should make certain that <u>he or she</u> has a ticket.

NOTE: Be careful not to use *they* or *their* to refer to a singular antecedent.

Drivers
~~Any driver~~ caught speeding should have their driving privileges suspended.

✔ ELIMINATING SEXIST LANGUAGE

SEXIST USAGE	POSSIBLE REVISIONS
1. Mankind	People, human beings
Man's accomplishments	Human accomplishments
Man-made	Synthetic
2. Female engineer (lawyer, accountant, etc.), male model	Engineer (lawyer, accountant, etc.), model

continued on the following page

continued from the previous page

SEXIST USAGE	POSSIBLE REVISIONS
3. Policeman/woman Salesman/woman/girl Businessman/woman	Police officer Salesperson/representative Businessperson, executive
4. <u>Everyone</u> should complete <u>his</u> application by Tuesday.	Everyone should complete <u>his or her</u> application by Tuesday. <u>All students</u> should complete <u>their</u> applications by Tuesday.

PART 4

UNDERSTANDING PUNCTUATION

CHAPTER 15

END PUNCTUATION

15a Using Periods

Use a period to signal the end of most sentences, including indirect questions.

Something is rotten in Denmark.

They wondered whether the water was safe to drink.

Also use periods in most abbreviations.

Mr. Spock	Aug.	Dr. Livingstone
9 p.m.	etc.	vol. 23

If an abbreviation ends the sentence, do not add another period.

He promised to be there at 6 a.m.

However, add a question mark if the sentence is a question.

Did he arrive at 6 p.m.?

If the abbreviation falls *within* a sentence, use normal punctuation after the period.

He promised to be there at 6 p.m., but he forgot.

ABBREVIATIONS WITHOUT PERIODS

In general, periods are omitted from abbreviations in full or small caps but retained in lowercase abbreviations (except in scientific style). *U.S.* retains the periods. Periods are retained in letters that stand for peoples' names (E. B. White).

MD   RN   CE

Familiar abbreviations of names of corporations or government agencies and scientific and technical terms do not require periods.

CD-ROM   NYU   DNA   CIA   WCAU-FM

continued on the following page

continued from the previous page

Acronyms—new words formed from the initial letters or first few letters of a series of words—do not include periods.

hazmat   AIDS   NAFTA   CAT scan

Clipped forms (commonly accepted shortened forms of words, such as *gym, dorm, math,* and *fax*) do not use periods.

Postal abbreviations do not include periods.

TX   CA   MS   PA   FL   NY

Use periods to mark divisions in dramatic and poetic references.

Hamlet 2.2.1–5 (act, scene, lines)
Paradise Lost 7.163–167 (book, lines)

ELECTRONIC ADDRESSES

Periods, along with other punctuation marks (such as slashes and colons), are used in electronic addresses (URLs).

g.mckay@smu.edu
http://www.nwu.org/nwu

NOTE: When you type an electronic address, do not end it with a period or add spaces after periods within the address.

15b Using Question Marks

Use a question mark to signal the end of a direct question.

Who was that masked man?

Use a question mark in parentheses to indicate that a date or number is uncertain.

Aristophanes, the Greek playwright, was born in 448 (?) BC and died in 380 (?) BC.

EDITING MISUSED QUESTION MARKS

Use a period, not a question mark, with an indirect question.

The personnel officer asked whether he knew how to type~~?~~.

Do not use a question mark to convey sarcasm. Instead, suggest your attitude through your choice of words.

I refused his~~ ~~generous ~~(?)~~ offer.
         not very

15c   Using Exclamation Points

An exclamation point is used to signal the end of an emotional or emphatic statement, an emphatic interjection, or a forceful command.

Remember the Maine!

"No! Don't leave!," he cried.

EDITING MISUSED EXCLAMATION POINTS

Except for when you are recording dialogue, do not use exclamation points in college writing. Even in informal writing, use exclamation points sparingly.

CHAPTER 16

THE COMMA

16a Setting Off Independent Clauses

Use a comma when you form a compound sentence by link-
See ing two independent clauses with a **coordinating conjunction**
A1.7 *(and, but, or, nor, for, yet, so)* or a pair of **correlative conjunctions**.

The House approved the bill, <u>but</u> the Senate rejected it.

<u>Either</u> the hard drive is full, <u>or</u> the modem is too slow.

NOTE: You may omit the comma if two clauses connected by a
coordinating conjunction are very short: Love it or leave it.

16b Setting Off Items in a Series

Use commas between items in a series of three or more **coordinate elements** (words, phrases, or clauses joined by a coordinating conjunction).

Chipmunk, *raccoon*, and *Mugwump* are Native American
words.

You may pay <u>by check</u>, <u>with a credit card</u>, or <u>in cash</u>.

<u>Brazilians speak Portuguese</u>, <u>Colombians speak Spanish</u>,
and <u>Haitians speak French and Creole</u>.

NOTE: To avoid ambiguity, always use a comma before the coordinating conjunction that separates the last two items in a
series.

Do not use a comma to introduce or to close a series.

Three important criteria are, fat content, salt content, and
taste.

The provinces Quebec, Ontario, and Alberta, are in Canada.

Use a comma between items in a series of two or more **coordinate adjectives**—adjectives that modify the same word or
word group—unless they are joined by a conjunction.

She brushed her <u>long</u>, <u>shining</u> hair.

The baby was <u>tired</u> and <u>cranky</u> and <u>wet</u>. (no comma required)

✅ CHECKLIST: PUNCTUATING ADJECTIVES IN A SERIES

✔ If you can reverse the order of the adjectives or insert *and* between the adjectives without changing the meaning, the adjectives are coordinate, and you should use a comma.

She brushed her <u>long</u>, shining hair.
She brushed her <u>shining</u>, long hair.
She brushed her long [and] shining hair.

✔ If you cannot, the adjectives are not coordinate, and you should not use a comma.

Ten red balloons fell from the ceiling.
Red ten balloons fell from the ceiling.
Ten [and] red balloons fell from the ceiling.

NOTE: Numbers—such as *ten*—are not coordinate with other adjectives.

16c Setting Off Introductory Elements

An introductory dependent clause, verbal phrase, or prepositional phrase is generally set off from the rest of the sentence by a comma.

<u>Although the CIA used to call undercover agents *penetration agents*</u>, they now routinely refer to them as *moles*. (dependent clause)

<u>Pushing onward</u>, Scott struggled toward the South Pole. (verbal phrase)

<u>During the Depression</u>, movie attendance rose. (prepositional phrase)

If the clause or phrase is short, you may omit the comma—*provided that the sentence will be clear without it.*

<u>When I exercise</u> I drink plenty of water.

<u>After the exam</u> I took a four-hour nap.

TRANSITIONAL WORDS AND PHRASES

When a **transitional word or phrase** begins a sentence, it is usually set off with a comma.

However , any plan that is enacted must be fair.

In other words , we cannot act hastily.

16d Setting Off Nonessential Material

Use commas to set off nonessential material whether it appears at the beginning, in the middle, or at the end of a sentence.

(1) Nonrestrictive Modifiers

Do *not* use commas to set off **restrictive modifiers,** which supply information essential to the meaning of the word or word group they modify. However, *do* use commas to set off **nonrestrictive modifiers,** which supply information that is not essential to the meaning of the word or word group they modify.

RESTRICTIVE (no commas):
Actors who have inflated egos are often insecure. (Only those actors with inflated egos—not all actors—are insecure.)

NONESTRICTIVE (commas required):
Actors , who have inflated egos, are often insecure. (*All* actors—not just those with inflated egos—are insecure.)

In the following examples, commas set off only nonrestrictive modifiers—those that supply nonessential information—but not restrictive modifiers, which supply essential information.

Adjective Clauses
RESTRICTIVE: Speaking in public is something that most people fear.

NONRESTRICTIVE: He ran for the bus , which was late as usual.

Prepositional Phrases
RESTRICTIVE: The man with the gun demanded their money.

NONRESTRICTIVE: The clerk , with a nod , dismissed me.

Verbal Phrases
RESTRICTIVE: The candidates running for mayor have agreed to a debate.

NONRESTRICTIVE: The marathoner ‸ running his fastest ‸ beat his previous record.

Appositives
RESTRICTIVE: The film *Citizen Kane* made Orson Welles famous.

NONRESTRICTIVE: *Citizen Kane*, Orson Welles's first film ‸ made him famous.

✔ CHECKLIST: RESTRICTIVE AND NONRESTRICTIVE MODIFIERS

To determine whether a modifier is restrictive or nonrestrictive, answer these questions.

✔ Is the modifier essential to the meaning of the noun it modifies (*The man with the gun*, not just any man)? If so, it is restrictive and does not take commas.

✔ Is the modifier introduced by *that* (*something that most people fear*)? If so, it is restrictive. *That* cannot introduce a nonrestrictive clause.

✔ Can you delete the relative pronoun without causing ambiguity or confusion (*something [that] most people fear*)? If so, the clause is restrictive.

✔ Is the appositive more specific than the noun that precedes it (*the film* Citizen Kane)? If so, it is restrictive.

USING COMMAS WITH *THAT* AND *WHICH*

That is used to introduce only restrictive clauses; *which* can be used to introduce both restrictive and nonrestrictive clauses. Many writers, however, prefer to use *which* only to introduce nonrestrictive clauses.

(2) Transitional Words and Phrases

<u>Transitional words and phrases</u> qualify, clarify, and make connections. However, they are not essential to meaning. For

See 2b

this reason, they are always set off by commas when they interrupt or come at the end of a clause (as well as when they begin a
sentence).

> The Outward Bound program, for example, is extremely
> safe.

> Other programs are not so safe, however.

TRANSITIONAL WORDS AND PHRASES

When a transitional word or phrase joins two independent clauses, it must be preceded by a semicolon and
followed by a comma.

Laughter is the best medicine; of course, penicillin
also comes in handy sometimes.

---

(3) Contradictory Phrases and Absolute Phrases

A phrase that expresses a contradiction is usually set off by
commas.

> This medicine is taken after meals, never on an empty stomach.

> Mark McGwire, not Sammy Sosa, was the first to break
> Roger Maris's home-run record.

An **absolute phrase,** which usually consists of a noun plus a
participle, is always set off by commas from the sentence it
modifies.

> His fear increasing, he waited to enter the haunted house.

(4) Miscellaneous Nonessential Elements

Other nonessential elements usually set off by commas include tag questions, names in direct address, mild interjections,
and *yes* and *no.*

> This is your first day on the job, isn't it?

> I wonder, Mr. Honeywell, whether Mr. Albright deserves a
> raise.

> Well, it's about time.

> Yes, we have no bananas.

16e Using Commas in Other Conventional Contexts

(1) With Direct Quotations

In most cases, use commas to set off a direct quotation from the **identifying tag** (*he said, she answered,* and so on).

Emerson said, "I greet you at the beginning of a great career."

"I greet you at the beginning of a great career," Emerson said.

"I greet you," Emerson said, "at the beginning of a great career."

When the identifying tag comes between two complete sentences, however, the tag is introduced by a comma but followed by a period.

"Winning isn't everything," Vince Lombardi said. "It's the only thing."

(2) With Titles or Degrees Following a Name

Michael Crichton, M.D., wrote *Jurassic Park.*

Hamlet, Prince of Denmark, is Shakespeare's most famous character.

(3) In Dates and Addresses

On August 30, 1983, the space shuttle *Challenger* was launched.

Her address is 600 West End Avenue, New York, NY 10024.

NOTE: When only the month and year are given, no commas are used (May 1968). No comma separates the street number from the street or the state name from the zip code.

16f Using Commas to Prevent Misreading

In some cases, a comma is used to prevent ambiguity. For example, consider the following sentence.

Those who can, sprint the final lap.

Without the comma, *can* appears to be an auxiliary verb ("Those who can sprint. . . ."), and the sentence seems incomplete. The comma tells readers to pause and thereby prevents confusion.

Also use a comma to acknowledge the omission of a repeated word, usually a verb, and to separate words repeated consecutively.

Pam carried the box; Tim, the suitcase.

Everything bad that could have happened, happened.

16g Editing Misused Commas

Do not use commas in the following situations.

(1) To Set Off Restrictive Modifiers

The film, Malcolm X, was directed by Spike Lee.

They planned a picnic, in the park.

(2) Between a Subject and Its Predicate

A woman with dark red hair, opened the door.

(3) Between a Verb and an Indirect Quotation or Indirect Question

General Douglas MacArthur vowed, that he would return.

The landlord asked, if we would sign a two-year lease.

(4) In Compounds That Are Not Composed of Independent Clauses

During the 1400s plagues, and pestilence were common. (compound subject)

Many women 35 and older are returning to college, and tend to be good students. (compound predicate)

(5) Before a Dependent Clause at the End of a Sentence

Jane Addams founded Hull House, because she wanted to help Chicago's poor.

CHAPTER 17

THE SEMICOLON

The **semicolon** is used only between items of equal grammatical rank: two independent clauses, two phrases, and so on.

17a Separating Independent Clauses

Use a semicolon between closely related independent clauses that convey parallel or contrasting information but are not joined by a coordinating conjunction.

> Paul Revere's *The Boston Massacre* is an early example of American protest art; Edward Hicks's later "primitive" paintings are socially conscious art with a religious strain.

CLOSE-UP

USING SEMICOLONS

Using only a comma or no punctuation at all between independent clauses creates a **comma splice** or a **fused sentence**.

See Ch. 3

Use a semicolon between two independent clauses when the second clause is introduced by a transitional word or phrase (the transitional element is followed by a comma).

> Thomas Jefferson brought two hundred vanilla beans and a recipe for vanilla ice cream back from France; thus, he gave America its all-time favorite ice cream flavor.

17b Separating Items in a Series

Use semicolons between items in a series when one or more of these items include commas.

> Three papers are posted on the bulletin board outside the building: a description of the exams; a list of appeal procedures for students who fail; and an employment ad from an automobile factory, addressed specifically to candidates whose appeals are turned down. (Andrea Lee, *Russian Journal*)

Laramie, Wyoming; Wyoming, Delaware; and Delaware, Ohio, were three of the places they visited.

17c Editing Misused Semicolons

Do not use semicolons in the following situations.

(1) Between a Dependent and an Independent Clause

Because drugs can now suppress the body's immune reaction, fewer organ transplants are rejected.

(2) To Introduce a List

Despite the presence of CNN and FOX News, the evening news remains a battleground for the three major television networks: CBS, NBC, and ABC.

(3) To Introduce a Direct Quotation

Marie Antoinette may not have said, "Let them eat cake."

CHAPTER 18

THE APOSTROPHE

Use an apostrophe to form the possessive case, to indicate omissions in contractions, and to form certain plurals.

18a Forming the Possessive Case

The possessive case indicates ownership. In English, the possessive case of nouns and indefinite pronouns is indicated either with a phrase that includes the word *of* (the hands *of* the clock) or with an apostrophe and, in most cases, an *s* (the clock's hands).

(1) Singular Nouns and Indefinite Pronouns

To form the possessive case of singular nouns and indefinite pronouns, add 's.

"The Monk's Tale" is one of Chaucer's *Canterbury Tales.*

When we would arrive was anyone's guess.

NOTE: With some singular nouns that end in -*s*, pronouncing the possessive ending as a separate syllable can sound awkward. In such cases, it is acceptable to use just an apostrophe: Aristophanes' *Lysistrata.*

(2) Plural Nouns

To form the possessive case of regular plural nouns (those that end in -*s* or -*es*), add only an apostrophe.

Laid-off employees received two weeks' severance pay and three months' medical benefits.

The Lopezes' three children are triplets.

To form the possessive case of nouns that have irregular plurals, add 's.

The Children's Hour is a play by Lillian Hellman.

(3) Compound Nouns or Groups of Words

To form the possessive case of compound words or of groups of words, add 's to the last word.

The Secretary of State's resignation was accepted under protest.

This is someone else's responsibility.

(4) Two or More Items

To indicate individual ownership of two or more items, add 's to each item.

> Ernest Hemingway's and Gertrude Stein's writing styles have some similarities.

To indicate joint ownership, add 's only to the last item.

> We studied Lewis and Clark's expedition.

APOSTROPHES WITH PLURAL NOUNS AND PERSONAL PRONOUNS

Do not use apostrophes with plural nouns that are not possessive.

> The Thompsons are out.

> These down vests are very warm.

> The Philadelphia Seventy Sixers have some outstanding players.

Do not use apostrophes to form the possessive case of personal pronouns.

> This ticket must be yours or hers.

> The next turn is theirs.

> The doll lost its right eye.

> The next great moment in history is ours.

Be especially careful not to confuse **contractions** (which always include apostrophes) with the possessive forms of personal pronouns (which never include apostrophes).

Contraction	*Possessive Form*
Who's on first?	Whose book is this?
They're playing our song.	Their team is winning.
It's raining.	Its paws were muddy.
You're a real pal.	Your résumé is very impressive.

See
18b

18b   Indicating Omissions in Contractions

Apostrophes replace omitted letters in contractions that combine a pronoun and a verb (*he + will = he'll*) or the elements of a verb phrase (*do + not = don't*).

FREQUENTLY USED CONTRACTIONS

it's (it is)	let's (let us)
we've (we have)	isn't (is not)
they're (they are)	wouldn't (would not)
we'll (we will)	don't (do not)
I'm (I am)	won't (will not)

In informal writing, an apostrophe may also be used to represent the century in a year: Class of '97, the '60s. In college writing, however, write out the year in full.

18c   Forming Plurals

Do not add *'s* to form a plural unless the result is confusing.

FORMING PLURALS: APOSTROPHE OR NOT?

Plurals of Words Referred to as Words

The supervisor would accept no *ifs, ands,* or *buts.*

Plurals of Lowercase Letters

The Italian language has no *j*'s or *k*'s.

Do not use an apostrophe to form the plurals of numbers or capital letters.

How many Bs did she receive?

There are three 4s in the equation.

NOTE: <u>Elements spoken of as themselves</u> (letters or words) are set in italic type; the plural ending, however, is not.

See 23c

CHAPTER 19

QUOTATION MARKS

Use quotation marks to set off brief passages of quoted speech or writing, to set off titles, and to set off words used in special ways. Do not use quotation marks when quoting long passages of prose or poetry.

19a Setting Off Quoted Speech or Writing

When you quote a word, phrase, or brief passage of someone's speech or writing, enclose the quoted material in a pair of quotation marks.

> Gloria Steinem observed, "We are becoming the men we once hoped to marry."

> Galsworthy describes Aunt Juley as "prostrated by the blow." (p. 329). (Note that the parenthetical documentation follows the end punctuation.)

Special rules govern the punctuation of a quotation when it is used with an **identifying tag**—a phrase (such as *he said*) that identifies the speaker or writer.

(1) Identifying Tag in the Middle of a Quoted Passage

Use a pair of commas to set off an identifying tag that interrupts a quoted passage.

> "In the future," pop artist Andy Warhol once said, "everyone will be world famous for fifteen minutes."

If the identifying tag follows a completed sentence but the quoted passage continues, use a period after the tag, and begin the new sentence with a capital letter and quotation marks.

> "Be careful," Erin warned. "Reptiles can be tricky."

(2) Identifying Tag at the Beginning of a Quoted Passage

Use a comma after an identifying tag that introduces quoted speech or writing.

> The Raven repeated, "Nevermore."

Use a <u>**colon**</u> instead of a comma before a quotation if the ^{See} identifying tag is a complete sentence. ^{20a}

She gave her final answer**:** "No."

(3) Identifying Tag at the End of a Quoted Passage

Use a comma to set off a quotation from an identifying tag that follows it.

"Be careful out there**,**" the sergeant warned.

If the quotation ends with a question mark or an exclamation point, use that punctuation mark instead of the comma. In this situation, the tag begins with a lowercase letter even though it follows end punctuation.

"Is Ankara the capital of Turkey**?**" she asked.

"Oh boy**!**" he cried.

NOTE: Commas and periods are always placed inside quotation marks. For information on placement of other punctuation marks with quotation marks, see **19d.**

NOTE: When you record **dialogue** (conversation between two or more people), enclose the quoted words in quotation marks. Begin a new paragraph each time a new speaker is introduced. When you are quoting several paragraphs of dialogue by one speaker, begin each new paragraph with quotation marks. However, use closing quotation marks only at the end of the entire passage (not at the end of each paragraph).

QUOTING LONG PROSE PASSAGES

A **long prose passage** (more than eight lines or one hundred words) is usually not enclosed in quotation marks. Instead, set it off by indenting the entire passage ½ inch (about ten spaces) from the left-hand margin. Leave space above and below the quoted passage. Introduce the passage with a colon if the introductory text is a phrase. A comma may also be used. If the introductory text is a sentence, use a colon or a period.

The following portrait of Aunt Juley illustrates several of the devices Galsworthy uses throughout <u>The Forsyte</u>

continued on the following page

87

continued from the previous page

<u>Saga</u>, such as a journalistic detachment, a sense of the grotesque, and an ironic stance:

> Aunt Juley stayed in her room, prostrated by the blow. Her face, discoloured by tears, was divided into compartments by the little ridges of pouting flesh which had swollen with emotion. . . . Her warm heart could not bear the thought that Ann was lying there so cold. (329)

Similar characterizations appear throughout the novel although not every passage includes so many different stylistic devices.

When quoting a long prose passage, retain the paragraphing of the original. If the first sentence of the quoted passage does not begin a paragraph in the source, do not indent it.

Shorter passages may be set off for emphasis.

QUOTING POETRY

Treat one line of poetry like a short prose passage: enclose it in quotation marks and run it into the text. If you quote two or three lines of poetry, separate the lines with **slashes**, and run the quotation into the text. If you quote more than three lines of poetry, set them off like a long prose passage. (For special emphasis, you may set off fewer lines in this way.) Be sure to reproduce *exactly* the spelling, capitalization, and indentation of the quoted lines.

See 20e

Wilfred Owen, a poet who was killed in action in World War I, expressed the horrors of war with vivid imagery:

> Bent double, like old beggars under sacks.
> Knock-kneed, coughing like hags, we cursed
>   through sludge.
> Till on the haunting flares we turned our backs
> And towards our distant rest began to trudge. (1–4)

19b Setting Off Titles

<u>Titles</u> of short works and titles of parts of long works are See 23a enclosed in quotation marks. Other titles are italicized.

TITLES REQUIRING QUOTATION MARKS

Articles in Magazines, Newspapers, and Professional Journals
"Why Johnny Can't Write" (*Newsweek*)

Essays, Short Stories, Short Poems, and Songs
"Fenimore Cooper's Literary Offenses"
"Flying Home"
"The Road Not Taken"
"The Star-Spangled Banner"

Chapters or Sections of Books
"Miss Sharp Begins to Make Friends" (Chapter 10 of *Vanity Fair*)

Episodes of Radio or Television Series
"Lucy Goes to the Hospital" (*I Love Lucy*)

19c Setting Off Words Used in Special Ways

Enclose a word used in a special or unusual way in quotation marks. (If you use *so-called* before the word, do not use quotation marks as well.)

It was clear that adults approved of children who were "readers," but it was not at all clear why this was so. (Annie Dillard)

Also enclose a **coinage**—an invented word—in quotation marks.

After the twins were born, the minivan became a "baby-mobile."

19d Using Quotation Marks with Other Punctuation

Place quotation marks *after* the comma or period at the end of a quotation.

Many, like poet Robert Frost, think about "the road not taken," but not many have taken "the one less traveled by."

Place quotation marks *before* a semicolon or colon at the end of a quotation.

Students who do not pass the test receive "certificates of completion"; those who pass are awarded diplomas.

Taxpayers were pleased with the first of the candidate's promised "sweeping new reforms": a balanced budget.

If a question mark, exclamation point, or dash is part of the quotation, place the quotation marks *after* the punctuation.

"Who's there?" she demanded.

"Stop!" he cried.

"Should we leave now, or —" Vicki paused, unable to continue.

If a question mark, exclamation point, or dash is not part of the quotation, place the quotation marks *before* the punctuation.

Did you finish reading "The Black Cat"?

Whatever you do, don't yell "Uncle"!

The first story—Updike's "*A & P*"—provoked discussion.

QUOTATIONS WITHIN QUOTATIONS

Use *single* quotation marks to enclose a quotation within a quotation.

Claire noted, "Liberace always said, 'I cried all the way to the bank.'"

Also use single quotation marks within a quotation to indicate a title that would normally be enclosed in double quotation marks.

I think what she said was, "Play it, Sam. Play 'As Time Goes By.'"

Use double quotation marks around quotations or titles within a **long prose passage**.

See
19a

19e　Editing Misused Quotation Marks

Do not use quotation marks to set off indirect quotations (someone else's written or spoken words that are not quoted exactly).

Freud wondered ⁓what women wanted.⁓

Do not use quotation marks to set off slang or technical terms.

Dawn is ⁓into⁓ running.

⁓Biofeedback⁓ is sometimes used to treat migraines.

CLOSE-UP　TITLES OF YOUR OWN PAPERS

Do not use quotation marks (or italics) to set off the title of your own paper.

CHAPTER 20

OTHER PUNCTUATION MARKS

20a Using Colons

The **colon** is a strong punctuation mark that points readers ahead to the rest of the sentence. When a colon introduces a list or series, explanatory material, or a quotation, it must be preceded by a complete sentence.

(1) Introducing Lists or Series

Use colons to set off lists or series, including those introduced by phrases like *the following* or *as follows.*

> Waiting tables requires three skills: memory, speed, and balance.

(2) Introducing Explanatory Material

Use colons to introduce material that explains, exemplifies, or summarizes.

> She had one dream: to play professional basketball.

Sometimes a colon separates two independent clauses, the second illustrating or clarifying the first.

> The survey presents an interesting finding: Americans do not trust the news media.

 USING COLONS

When a complete sentence follows a colon, the sentence may begin with either a capital or a lowercase letter. However, if the sentence is a quotation, the first word is always capitalized (unless it was not capitalized in the source).

(3) Introducing Quotations

See 19a

When you quote a **long prose passage**, introduce it with a colon. Also use a colon before a short quotation when it is introduced by a complete independent clause.

> With dignity, Bartleby repeated the words again: "I prefer not to."

OTHER CONVENTIONAL USES OF COLONS

To Separate Titles from Subtitles
Family Installments: *Memories of Growing Up Hispanic*

To Separate Minutes from Hours
6:15 a.m.

To Separate Chapter and Verse in Biblical References
Judges 4:14

After Salutations in <u>Business Letters</u>
Dear Dr. Evans:

See 35a

To Separate Place of Publication from Name of Publisher in a <u>Bibliography</u>
Boston: Heinle, 2003.

See 31a

---

(4) Editing Misused Colons

Do not use colons after expressions such as *namely, for example, such as,* or *that is.*

The Eye Institute treats patients with a wide variety of conditions, such as∕ myopia, glaucoma, and cataracts.

Do not place colons between verbs and their objects or complements or between prepositions and their objects.

James Michener wrote∕ *Hawaii, Centennial, Space,* and *Poland.*

Hitler's armies marched through∕ the Netherlands, Belgium, and France.

20b Using Dashes

(1) Setting Off Nonessential Material

Like commas, **dashes** can set off <u>nonessential material</u>, but unlike commas, dashes call attention to the material they set off. When you type, you indicate a dash with two unspaced hyphens (which most word processing programs will convert to a dash).

See 16d

For emphasis, you may use dashes to set off explanations, qualifications, examples, definitions, and appositives.

Neither of the boys—both nine-year-olds—had any history of violence.

Too many parents learn the dangers of swimming pools the hard way—after their toddler has drowned.

(2) Introducing a Summary

Use a dash to introduce a statement that summarizes a list or series that appears before it.

"Study hard," "Respect your elders," "Don't talk with your mouth full"—Sharon had often heard her parents say these things.

(3) Indicating an Interruption

In dialogue, a dash may indicate a hesitation or an unfinished thought.

"I think—no, I know—this is the worst day of my life," Julie sighed.

(4) Editing Overused Dashes

Because too many dashes can make a passage seem disorganized and out of control, dashes should not be overused.

Registration was a nightmare. ~~most~~ Most of the courses I wanted to take—geology and conversational Spanish, for instance—met at inconvenient times—or were closed by the time I tried to sign up for them.

20c   Using Parentheses

(1) Setting Off Nonessential Material

Use parentheses to enclose material that is relatively unimportant in a sentence—for example, material that expands, clarifies, illustrates, or supplements.

In some European countries (notably Sweden and France), superb daycare is offered at little or no cost to parents.

Also use parentheses to set off digressions and afterthoughts.

Last Sunday we went to the new stadium (it was only half-filled) to see the game.

When a complete sentence set off by parentheses falls within another sentence, it should not begin with a capital letter or end with a period.

The area is so cold (temperatures average in the low twenties) that it is virtually uninhabitable.

If the parenthetical sentence does *not* fall within another sentence, however, it must begin with a capital letter and end with appropriate punctuation.

The region is very cold. (Temperatures average in the low twenties.)

(2) Using Parentheses in Other Situations

Use parentheses around letters and numbers that identify points on a list, dates, cross references, and documentation.

All reports must include the following components: (1) an opening summary, (2) a background statement, and (3) a list of conclusions.

Russia defeated Sweden in the Great Northern War (1700–1721).

Other scholars also make this point (see p. 54).

One critic has called the novel "puerile" (Arvin 72).

 Using Brackets

Brackets within quotations tell readers that the enclosed words are yours and not those of your source. You can bracket an explanation, a clarification, a correction, or an opinion.

"Even at Princeton he [F. Scott Fitzgerald] felt like an outsider."

If a quotation contains an error, indicate that the error is not yours by following the error with the italicized Latin word *sic* ("thus") in brackets.

"The octopuss [sic] is a cephalopod mollusk with eight arms."

NOTE: Use brackets to indicate parentheses that fall within parentheses.

> ### USING BRACKETS TO EDIT QUOTATIONS
>
> Use brackets to indicate changes that enable you to fit a **quotation** smoothly into your sentence. Use **ellipses** to indicate that you have omitted words from a quotation.

See 30a1
See 20f

 Using Slashes

(1) Separating One Option from Another

The either / or fallacy is a common error in logic.

Writer / director M. Night Shyamalan spoke at the film festival.

Note that in this case there is no space before or after the slash.

(2) Separating Lines of Poetry Run into the Text

The poet James Schevill writes, "I study my defects */* And learn how to perfect them."

In this case, leave one space before and one space after the slash.

20f Using Ellipses

Use an **ellipsis**—three *spaced* periods—to indicate that you have omitted words (or even entire sentences) from a quotation. When deleting material from a quotation, be very careful not to change the meaning of the original passage.

> **ORIGINAL:** "When I was a young man, being anxious to distinguish myself, I was perpetually starting new propositions." (Samuel Johnson)

> **WITH OMISSION:** "When I was a young man, ... I was perpetually starting new propositions."

Note that when you delete words immediately after an internal punctuation mark (such as a comma), you retain the punctuation before the ellipsis.

When you delete words *at the end of a sentence,* use the sentence's period or other end punctuation followed by the ellipsis.

> According to humorist Dave Barry, "from outer space Europe appears to be shaped like a large ketchup stain...."

NOTE: Never begin a quoted passage with an ellipsis.

When you delete material from a quotation of more than one sentence, place the end punctuation before the ellipsis.

Deletion from Middle of One Sentence to End of Another

> According to Donald Hall, "Everywhere one meets the idea that reading is an activity desirable in itself. . . . People surround the idea of reading with piety and do not take into account the purpose of reading."

Deletion from Middle of One Sentence to Middle of Another

> "When I was a young man, . . . I found that generally what was new was false." (Samuel Johnson)

NOTE: An ellipsis in the middle of a quoted passage can indicate the omission of a word, a sentence or two, or even a whole paragraph or more.

 USING ELLIPSES

If a quotation ending with an ellipsis is followed by parenthetical documentation, the final punctuation *follows* the documentation.

As Jarman argues, "Compromise was impossible ... " (p. 161).

PART 5

SPELLING AND MECHANICS

CHAPTER 21

SPELLING

21a Understanding Spelling and Pronunciation

Because pronunciation in English often provides few clues to spelling, you must memorize the spellings of many words and use a dictionary or spell checker regularly.

(1) Vowels in Unstressed Positions

Many unstressed vowels sound exactly alike. For instance, the unstressed vowels *a, e,* and *i* are impossible to distinguish by pronunciation alone in the suffixes -*able* and -*ible,* -*ance* and -*ence,* and -*ant* and -*ent.*

comfort<u>able</u>	brilli<u>ance</u>	serv<u>ant</u>
compat<u>ible</u>	excell<u>ence</u>	independ<u>ent</u>

(2) Silent Letters

Some English words contain silent letters, such as the *b* in *climb* and the *t* in *mortgage.*

ai<u>s</u>le	de<u>p</u>ot
condem<u>n</u>	<u>k</u>night
des<u>c</u>end	<u>p</u>neumonia

(3) Words That Are Often Pronounced Carelessly

Words like the following are often misspelled because when we pronounce them, we add, omit, or transpose letters.

can<u>d</u>idate	nuc<u>l</u>ear	recognize
environ<u>m</u>ent	lib<u>r</u>ary	supposed to
Feb<u>r</u>uary	quan<u>t</u>ity	use<u>d</u> to

(4) Homophones

Homophones are words—such as *accept* and *except*—that are pronounced alike but spelled differently. For a list of homophones, along with their meanings and sentences illustrating their use, consult **Appendix B,** "Usage Review."

21b Learning Spelling Rules

Memorizing a few reliable spelling rules can help you overcome some of the problems caused by inconsistencies between pronunciation and spelling.

(1) The *ie/ei* Combinations

Use *i* before *e* (*belief, chief*) except after *c* (*ceiling, receive*) or when pronounced *ay*, as in *neighbor* or *weigh*. **Exceptions:** *either, neither, foreign, leisure, weird,* and *seize.* In addition, if the *ie* combination is not pronounced as a unit, the rule does not apply: *atheist, science.*

(2) Doubling Final Consonants

The only words that double their consonants before a suffix that begins with a vowel (*-ed* or *-ing*) are those that pass the following three tests.

1. They have one syllable or are stressed on the last syllable.
2. They have only one vowel in the last syllable.
3. They end in a single consonant.

The word *tap* satisfies all three conditions: it has only one syllable, it has only one vowel (*a*), and it ends in a single consonant (*p*). Therefore, the final consonant doubles before a suffix beginning with a vowel (*tapped, tapping*).

(3) Silent *e* before a Suffix

When a suffix that begins with a consonant is added to a word ending in a silent *e*, the *e* is generally kept: *hope/hopeful.* **Exceptions:** *argument, truly, ninth, judgment,* and *abridgment.*

When a suffix that begins with a vowel is added to a word ending in a silent *e*, the *e* is generally dropped: *hope/hoping.* **Exceptions:** *changeable, noticeable,* and *courageous.*

(4) *y* before a Suffix

When a word ends in a consonant plus *y*, the *y* generally changes to an *i* when a suffix is added (*beauty + ful = beautiful*). The *y* is kept, however, when the suffix *-ing* is added (*tally + ing = tallying*) and in some one-syllable words (*dry + ness = dryness*).

When a word ends in a vowel plus *y*, the *y* is kept (*joy + ful = joyful*). **Exception:** *day + ly = daily.*

(5) *seed* Endings

Endings with the sound *seed* are nearly always spelled *cede*, as in *precede.* **Exceptions:** *supersede, exceed, proceed,* and *succeed.*

(6) *-able, -ible*

If the root of a word is itself a word, the suffix *-able* is most commonly used (*comfortable, agreeable*). If the root of a word is not a word, the suffix -*ible* is most often used (*compatible, incredible*).

(7) Plurals

Most nouns form plurals by adding *s*: *tortilla/tortillas, boat/boats*. There are, however, a number of exceptions.

- Some words ending in -*f* or -*fe* form plurals by changing the *f* to *v* and adding *es* or *s*: *life/lives, self/selves*. Others add just *s*: *belief/beliefs, safe/safes*.
- Most words that end in a consonant followed by *y* form plurals by changing the *y* to *i* and adding *es*: *baby/babies*. **Exceptions:** proper nouns such as *Kennedy* (plural *Kennedys*).
- Most words that end in a consonant followed by *o* add *es* to form the plural: *tomato/tomatoes, hero/heroes*. **Exceptions:** *silo/silos, piano/pianos, memo/memos, soprano/sopranos*.
- Words ending in -*s*, -*sh*, -*ch*, -*x*, and -*z* form plurals by adding *es*: *Jones/Joneses, rash/rashes, lunch/lunches, box/boxes, buzz/buzzes*. **Exceptions:** Some one-syllable words that end in -*s* or -*z* double their final consonants when forming plurals: *quiz/quizzes*.
- Hyphenated compound nouns whose first element is more important than the others form the plural with the first element: *sister-in-law/sisters-in-law*.
- Some words, especially those borrowed from Latin or Greek, keep their foreign plurals.

Singular	*Plural*
criterion	criteria
datum	data
memorandum	memoranda
stimulus	stimuli

RUNNING A SPELL CHECK

If you use a computer spell checker, remember that it will not identify a word that is spelled correctly but used incorrectly—*then* for *than* or *its* for *it's*, for example—or a typo that creates another word, such as *form* for *from*. Even after you run a spell check, you still need to proofread your papers .

CHAPTER 22

CAPITALIZATION

In addition to capitalizing the first word of a sentence (including a quoted sentence) and the pronoun *I*, always capitalize proper nouns and important words in titles.

22a Capitalizing Proper Nouns

Proper nouns—the names of specific persons, places, or things—are capitalized, and so are adjectives formed from proper nouns.

(1) Specific People's Names

Eleanor Roosevelt   Medgar Evers

Capitalize a title when it precedes a person's name or replaces the name (Senator Barbara Boxer, Dad). Do not capitalize titles that *follow* names or that refer to the general position, not to the particular person who holds it (Barbara Boxer, the senator), except for very high-ranking positions: President of the United States. Never capitalize a title denoting a family relationship when it follows an article or a possessive pronoun: an aunt, my uncle.

Capitalize titles or abbreviations of academic degrees, even when they follow a name: Dr. Benjamin Spock, Benjamin Spock, M.D.

(2) Names of Particular Structures, Special Events, Monuments, and so on

the *Titanic*   the World Series
the Brooklyn Bridge   Mount Rushmore

(3) Places and Geographical Regions

Saturn   the Straits of Magellan
Budapest   the Western Hemisphere

Capitalize *north, east, south,* and *west* when they denote particular geographical regions (the West), but not when they designate directions (west of town).

(4) Days of the Week, Months, and Holidays

Saturday	Rosh Hashanah
January	Ramadan

(5) Historical Periods and Events, Documents, and Names of Legal Cases

the Battle of Gettysburg	Romanticism
Brown v. Board of Education	the Treaty of Versailles

(6) Races, Ethnic Groups, Nationalities, and Languages

African American	Korean
Latino/Latina	Dutch

NOTE: When the words *black* and *white* refer to races, they have traditionally not been capitalized. Current usage is divided on whether to capitalize *black*.

(7) Religions and Their Followers; Sacred Books and Figures

Jews	the Talmud	Buddha
Islam	God	the Scriptures

(8) Specific Organizations

the New York Yankees	the American Bar Association
the League of Women Voters	the Anti-Defamation League

(9) Businesses, Government Agencies, and Other Institutions

Congress	Lincoln High School
the Environmental Protection Agency	the University of Maryland

(10) Brand Names and Words Formed from Them

Coke	Astroturf	Rollerblades	Post-it

(11) Specific Academic Courses and Departments

Sociology 201	Department of English

NOTE: Do not capitalize a general subject area (sociology, zoology) unless it is the name of a language (French).

(12) Adjectives Formed from Proper Nouns

Keynesian economics	Elizabethan era
Freudian slip	Shakespearean sonnet

When words derived from proper nouns have lost their special-ized meanings, do not capitalize them: *china* pattern, *french* fries.

22b Capitalizing Important Words in Titles

In general, capitalize all words in titles with the exception of articles (*a, an,* and *the*), prepositions, coordinating conjunctions, and the *to* in infinitives. If an article, preposition, or coordinating conjunction is the *first* or *last* word in the title or is otherwise stressed, do capitalize it. Except for proper names, do not capitalize the second element of a hyphenated term.

The Making of the Atomic Bomb
The Best and the Brightest
The Decline and Fall of the Roman Empire
Take-offs and Landings at LaGuardia
Life in the Twenty-first Century

CLOSE-UP

EDITING MISUSED CAPITALS

Do not capitalize the following.

- Seasons (summer, fall, winter, spring)
- Names of centuries (the twenty-first century)
- Names of general historical periods (the automobile age)
- Diseases and other medical terms (unless a proper noun is part of the name): mumps, smallpox, polio

CHAPTER 23

ITALICS

23a Setting Off Titles and Names

Use italics for the titles and names in the box below. All other titles are set off with **quotation marks**. Software programs are capitalized but not otherwise set off. Web sites and home pages are not italicized and not set within quotation marks.

See 19b

Word 2000   PowerPoint   urbanlegends.com

TITLES AND NAMES SET IN ITALICS

BOOKS: *David Copperfield, The Bluest Eye*

NEWSPAPERS: the *Washington Post,* the *Philadelphia Inquirer*

(Articles and names of cities are italicized only when they are part of a title.)

MAGAZINES AND JOURNALS: *Rolling Stone, Scientific American, PMLA*

ONLINE MAGAZINES AND JOURNALS *salon.com, theonion.com*

PAMPHLETS: *Common Sense*

FILMS: *Casablanca, Citizen Kane*

TELEVISION PROGRAMS: *Law & Order, 60 Minutes, The Simpsons*

RADIO PROGRAMS: *All Things Considered, A Prairie Home Companion*

LONG POEMS: *John Brown's Body, The Faerie Queen*

PLAYS: *Macbeth, A Raisin in the Sun*

LONG MUSICAL WORKS: *Rigoletto, Eroica*

PAINTINGS AND SCULPTURE: *Guernica, Pietà*

SHIPS: *Lusitania,* USS *Saratoga*

(SS, USS, and HMS are not italicized.)

continued on the following page

---

continued from the previous page

> **TRAINS:** *City of New Orleans, Orient Express*
>
> **AIRCRAFT:** *Hindenburg, Enola Gay*
>
> **SPACECRAFT:** *Challenger, Enterprise*
>
> (Only specific trains, aircraft, or spacecraft are italicized. Makes and types of trains, aircraft, or spacecraft are not italicized: Acela Express, Piper Cub, Gemini.)

NOTE: Names of sacred books, such as the Bible, and well-known documents, such as the Constitution and the Declaration of Independence, are neither italicized nor placed within quotation marks.

23b Setting Off Foreign Words and Phrases

Use italics to set off foreign words and phrases that have not become part of the English language.

"C'est la vie," Madeleine said when she saw the long line for basketball tickets.

Spirochaeta plicatilis is a corkscrew-like bacterium.

If you are not sure whether a foreign word has been assimilated into English, consult a dictionary.

23c Setting Off Elements Spoken of as Themselves and Terms Being Defined

Use italics to set off letters, numerals, and words that refer to the letters, numerals, and words themselves.

Is that a *p* or a *g?*

I forget the exact address, but I know it has a *3* in it.

Does *through* rhyme with *cough?*

Italics also set off words and phrases that you go on to define.

A *closet drama* is a play meant to be read, not performed.

NOTE: When you quote a dictionary definition, put the words you are defining in italics and the definition itself in quotation marks.

To *infer* means "to draw a conclusion"; to *imply* means "to suggest."

23d Using Italics for Emphasis

Italics can occasionally be used for emphasis.

Initially, poetry might be defined as a kind of language that says *more* and says it *more intensely* than does ordinary language. (Lawrence Perrine, *Sound and Sense*)

However, overuse of italics is distracting. Instead of italicizing, indicate emphasis with word choice and sentence structure.

CHAPTER 24

HYPHENS

Hyphens have two conventional uses: to break a word at the end of a typed or handwritten line and to link words in certain compounds.

24a Breaking a Word at the End of a Line

Word processing programs usually do not break a word at the end of a line; if the full word will not fit, it is brought down to the next line. Sometimes, however, you will want to break a word with a hyphen—for example, to fill in space at the end of a line. When you break a word at the end of a line, divide it only between syllables, consulting a dictionary if necessary. Never divide a word at the end of a page, and never hyphenate one-syllable words. In addition, never leave a single letter at the end of a line or carry only one or two letters to the next line.

See 24b

If you divide a **compound word** at the end of a line, put the hyphen between the elements of the compound (*snow-mobile*, not *snowmo-bile*).

 DIVIDING ELECTRONIC ADDRESSES

Do not insert a hyphen when dividing a long electronic address at the end of a line. (A hyphen at this point could confuse readers, making them think it is part of the address.) Instead, simply break the address before or after a slash or a period—or avoid the problem entirely by putting the entire address on one line.

24b Dividing Compound Words

A **compound word** is composed of two or more words. Some familiar compound words are always hyphenated: *no-hitter, helter-skelter.* Other compounds are always written as one word (*fireplace*) and others as two separate words (*bunk bed*). Your dictionary can tell you whether a particular compound requires a hyphen.

110

Dividing Compound Words

Hyphens are generally used in the following compounds.

(1) In Compound Adjectives

A **compound adjective** is a series of two or more words that function together as an adjective. When a compound adjective comes before the noun it modifies, use hyphens to join its elements.

The research team tried to use <u>nineteenth-century</u> technology to design a <u>space-age</u> project.

When a compound adjective *follows* the noun it modifies, do not use hyphens to join its elements.

The three government-operated programs were run smoothly, but the one that was not <u>government operated</u> was short of funds.

NOTE: A compound adjective formed with an adverb ending in -*ly* is not hyphenated even when it precedes the noun.

Many <u>upwardly mobile</u> families are on tight budgets.

Use **suspended hyphens**—hyphens followed by a space or by appropriate punctuation and a space—in a series of compounds that have the same principal elements.

The <u>three-, four-,</u> and <u>five-year-old</u> children ate lunch together.

(2) With Certain Prefixes or Suffixes

Use a hyphen between a prefix and a proper noun or adjective.

mid-July   pre-Columbian

Use a hyphen to connect the prefixes *all-, ex-, half-, quarter-, quasi-,* and *self-* and the suffix *-elect* to a noun.

ex-senator   self-centered
quarter-moon   president-elect

Also hyphenate to avoid certain hard-to-read combinations, such as two *i*'s (*semi-illiterate*) or more than two of the same consonant (*shell-less*).

(3) In Compound Numerals and Fractions

Hyphenate compounds that represent numbers below one hundred, even if they are part of a larger number.

the <u>twenty-first</u> century   three hundred <u>sixty-five</u> days

Also hyphenate the written form of a fraction when it modifies a noun.

a <u>two-thirds</u> share of the business

CHAPTER 25

ABBREVIATIONS

Generally speaking, **abbreviations** are not appropriate in college writing except in tables, charts, bibliographies, and lists. Some abbreviations are acceptable only in scientific, technical, or business writing or only in a particular discipline. If you have questions about the appropriateness of a particular abbreviation, check a style manual in your field.

25a Abbreviating Titles

Titles before and after proper names are usually abbreviated.

Mr. Homer Simpson   Rep. Chaka Fattah
Henry Kissinger, PhD   Dr. Martin Luther King Jr.

Do not, however, use an abbreviated title without a name.

The ~~Dr.~~ doctor diagnosed hepatitis.

25b Abbreviating Organization Names and Technical Terms

Well-known businesses and government, social, and civic organizations are commonly referred to by capitalized initials. These **abbreviations** fall into two categories: those in which the initials are pronounced as separate units (MTV) and **acronyms,** in which the initials are pronounced as a word (NATO).

See 15a

To save space, you may use accepted abbreviations for complex technical terms that are not well known, but be sure to spell out the full term the first time you mention it, followed by the abbreviation in parentheses.

Citrus farmers have been using ethylene dibromide (EDB), a chemical pesticide, for more than twenty years. Now, however, EDB has contaminated water supplies.

25c Abbreviating Dates, Times of Day, Temperatures, and Numbers

50 BC (BC follows the date)   AD 432 (AD precedes the date)
3:03 p.m. (lowercase)   180°F (Fahrenheit)

Always capitalize BC and AD (The alternatives BCE, for "before the Common Era," and CE, for "Common Era," are also capitalized.) The abbreviations a.m. and p.m. are used only when they are accompanied by numbers.

I'll see you in the ~~a.m.~~ morning.

Avoid the abbreviation *no.* except in technical writing, and then use it only before a specific number: *The unidentified substance was labeled no. 52.*

ABBREVIATIONS IN CHICAGO DOCUMENTATION STYLE

In general, abbreviations should not be used in the body of your paper but may be used in tables, notes, bibliographies, and parenthetical expressions. In bibliographies, Chicago documentation style permits abbreviations of journal names or publisher names as long as the names remain recognizable (Oxford Univ. Press, Houghton Mifflin). Also acceptable is the use of abbreviations that designate parts of editions of written works (chap. 3, sec. 7, 2nd ed.).

25d Editing Misused Abbreviations

In college writing, abbreviations are not used in the following cases.

(1) Latin Expressions

Poe wrote "The Gold Bug," "The Tell-Tale Heart," ~~etc.~~ and so on.

Many musicians (~~e.g.,~~ for example, Bruce Springsteen) have been influenced by Bob Dylan.

(2) Names of Days, Months, or Holidays

On ~~Sat., Dec.~~ Saturday, December 23, I started my ~~Xmas~~ Christmas shopping.

(3) Names of Streets and Places

He lives on Riverside ~~Dr.~~ Drive in ~~NYC.~~ New York City.

Exceptions: The abbreviations *U.S.* (*U.S. Coast Guard*), *St.* (*St. Albans*), *and Mt.* (*Mt. Etna*) are acceptable, as is *DC* in *Washington, DC.*

(4) Names of Academic Subjects

Psychology   literature
~~Psych.~~ and English ~~lit.~~ are required courses.

(5) Units of Measurement

In technical writing, some units of measurement are abbreviated when preceded by a numeral.

The hurricane had winds of 35 mph.

Our new Honda gets over 50 mpg.

In college writing, however, write out such expressions, and spell out words such as *inches, feet, years, miles, pints, quarts,* and *gallons.*

(6) Symbols

The symbols %, =, +, and # are acceptable in technical and scientific writing, but not in nontechnical college writing. The symbol *$* is acceptable before specific numbers ($15,000) but not as a substitute for the words *money* and *dollars.*

CHAPTER 26

NUMBERS

The guidelines in this chapter are based on the *Chicago Manual of Style,* fifteenth edition (2003). In general, Chicago style uses words for cardinal and ordinal numbers through one hundred; for round numbers; and for numbers at the beginning of a sentence; however, numerals and spelled-out numbers should generally not be used in the same passage.

26a Spelled-Out Numbers versus Numerals

The Hawaiian alphabet has only <u>twelve</u> letters.

Class size stabilized at <u>twenty-eight</u> students.

The subsidies are expected to total about <u>two million</u> dollars.

Maplewood is the <u>ninety-eighth</u> largest town in the state.

The professor prepared <u>125</u> questions for the history test.

The developer of the community purchased <u>300,000</u> doorknobs, <u>153,000</u> faucets, and <u>4,000</u> manhole covers.

NOTE: Chicago style normally spells out round numbers only (three hundred thousand, four thousand) and recommends treating numbers consistently within a single context.

CLOSE-UP   **NUMBERS AS SENTENCE OPENERS**

Never begin a sentence with a numeral. Spell out the number, or reword the sentence.

INCORRECT: 250 students are currently enrolled in History 101.

REVISED: Current enrollment in History 101 is 250 students.

26b Conventional Uses of Numerals

- **Addresses:** 111 Fifth Avenue, New York, NY 10003
- **Dates:** January 15, 1929   1914–1919
- **Exact Times:** 9:16   10 a.m. or 10:00 p.m.   ten o'clock
- **Exact Sums of Money:** $25.11 $6,752.00 or $6,752
  twenty-five cents
- **Divisions of Works:** Act 5   lines 17–28   page 42
  Judges 4:14
- **Decimals, Fractions, and Percentages:** 3.14   6¾
  53.8 percent
- **Measurements with Symbols or Abbreviations:** 32°F
  15 cm^3
- **Ratios and Statistics:** 20 to 1
- **Scores:** a lead of 6 to 0
- **Identification Numbers:** Route 66   Track 8   Channel 12

PART 6

WRITING WITH
SOURCES

CHAPTER 27

WRITING RESEARCH PAPERS

Research is the systematic investigation of a topic outside your own knowledge and experience. However, doing research means more than just reading about other people's ideas. When you undertake a research project, you become involved in a process that requires you to think critically, evaluating and interpreting the ideas explored in your sources and formulating ideas of your own.

Not so long ago, searching for source material meant spending long hours in the library flipping through card catalogs, examining heavy reference volumes, and hunting for books in the stacks. Technology, however, has dramatically changed the way research is conducted. The wiring of school and community libraries means that today, students and professionals engaged in research find themselves spending a great deal of time in front of a computer, particularly during the exploratory stage of the research process. Note, however, that although the way in which research materials are located and accessed has changed, the research process itself has not. Whether you are working with **electronic resources** (online catalogs, databases, the Internet), in the library or at your home computer, or **print sources** (books, journals, magazines), you need to follow a systematic process.

See 28a2

✔ CHECKLIST: THE RESEARCH PROCESS

- ✔ Choose a topic **(See 27a)**
- ✔ Do exploratory research and formulate a research question **(See 27b)**
- ✔ Assemble a working bibliography **(See 27c)**
- ✔ Develop a tentative thesis **(See 27d)**
- ✔ Do focused research **(See 27e)**
- ✔ Take notes **(See 27f)**
- ✔ Decide on a thesis **(See 27g)**
- ✔ Outline your paper **(See 27h1)**
- ✔ Draft your paper **(See 27h2)**
- ✔ Revise your paper **(See 27h3)**

27a Choosing a Topic

The first step in the research process is finding a topic to write about. In many cases, your instructor will help you to choose a topic, either by providing a list of suitable topics or by suggesting a general subject area—for example, a famous trial, an event that happened on the day of your birth, or the history of integration in your community. Even in these instances, you will still need to choose one of the topics or narrow the subject area—deciding, for example, on one trial, one event, or one problem.

If your instructor prefers that you select a topic on your own, you must consider a number of possible topics and weigh both their suitability for research and your interest in them. You decide on a topic for your research paper in much the same way in which you decide on a topic for a short essay: you read, brainstorm, talk to people, and ask questions. Specifically, you talk to friends and family members, co-workers, and perhaps your instructor; you read magazines and newspapers; you take stock of your interests; you consider possible topics suggested by your other courses—historical events, scientific developments, and so on; and, of course, you search the Internet. (Your search engine's **subject guides** can be particularly helpful as you look for a promising topic or narrow a broad subject.)

See 29a

As you look for a suitable topic, keep the following guidelines in mind.

✔ CHECKLIST: CHOOSING A RESEARCH TOPIC

✔ **Are you genuinely interested in your research topic?** Be sure the topic you select is one that will hold your interest.

✔ **Is your topic suitable for research?** Be sure your paper will not depend on your personal experiences or value judgments.

✔ **Is your topic too broad? too narrow?** Be sure the boundaries of your research topic are appropriate.

✔ **Can your topic be researched in a library to which you have access?** Be sure that your school library has the sources you need (or that you can access those sources on the Internet).

27b Doing Exploratory Research and Formulating a Research Question

Doing **exploratory research**—searching the Internet and looking through general reference works such as encyclopedias, bibliographies, and specialized dictionaries (either in print or online)—helps you to get an overview of your topic. Your goal is to formulate a **research question,** the question you want your research paper to answer. A research question helps you to decide which sources to seek out, which to examine first, which to examine in depth, and which to skip entirely. (The answer to your research question will be your paper's **thesis statement**.)   See 1c

27c Assembling a Working Bibliography

As soon as you start your exploratory research, you begin to assemble a **working bibliography** for your paper. (This working bibliography will be the basis for your **bibliography**, which will include all the sources you cite in your paper.)   See 32a

As you consider each potential source, record full and accurate bibliographic information—author, title, page numbers, and complete publication information—in a separate computer file designated "Bibliography" or, if you prefer, on individual index cards. (See Figures 1 and 2.) Keep records of interviews (including telephone and e-mail interviews), meetings, lectures, films, and electronic sources as well as of books and articles. For each source, include not only basic identifying details—such as

Author

Monroe Lee Billington and Roger Hadaway, editors

Title ———▶ *African Americans on the Western Frontier*

Publication ———▶ Boulder: University of Colorado Press, information 1998

Comments ———▶ This book contains a series of essays about African Americans and life on the western frontier. One essay is about Buffalo Soldiers and will be particularly helpful. It is written by one of the editors of the book, Monroe Lee Billington, and is entitled "Buffalo Soldiers in the American West, 1896–1898." It appears on pages 53–70.

Figure 1 Information for Working Bibliography (in computer file)

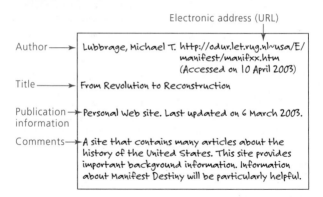

Electronic address (URL)

Author⟶ Lubbrage, Michael T. http://odur.let.rug.nl~usa/E/
                            manifest/manifxx.htm
                            (Accessed on 10 April 2003)

Title⟶ From Revolution to Reconstruction

Publication⟶ Personal Web site. Last updated on 6 March 2003.
information

Comments⟶ A site that contains many articles about the
            history of the United States. This site provides
            important background information. Information
            about Manifest Destiny will be particularly helpful.

*Figure 2 Information for Working Bibliography
          (on index card)*

the date of an interview, the call number of a library book, the
address (URL) of an Internet source, or the author of an article
accessed from a database—but also brief comments about the
kind of information the source contains, the amount of information offered, its relevance to your topic, and its limitations.

As you go about collecting sources and building your working bibliography, monitor the quality and relevance of all the
materials you examine. Making informed choices early in the
research process will save you a lot of time in the long run, so
don't collect a large number of sources first and assess their usefulness later. Before you check a book out of the library, photocopy a journal article, or download a text, take the time to
consider its relevance to your topic. Resist the temptation to
check out every book that mentions your subject, photocopy
page after page of marginally useful articles, or download material from every electronic source to which you have access. After
all, you will eventually have to read all these sources and take
detailed notes on them. If you have too many sources, you will
be overwhelmed, unable to remember why a particular idea or a
certain article seemed important. (For more on evaluating library sources, see **28b;** for guidelines on evaluating Internet
sources, see **29c.**)

27d Developing a Tentative Thesis

Your **tentative thesis** is a preliminary statement of what you
think your research will support. This statement, which you will
eventually refine into a **thesis statement**, should be the tentative answer to your research question.

See
27g

DEVELOPING A TENTATIVE THESIS

Subject Area	Topic	Research Question	Tentative Thesis
African Americans and U.S. History	Buffalo Soldiers and settlement of the western frontier.	What challenges did the Buffalo Soldiers face as they helped settlers move West?	Buffalo Soldiers were pioneers in the struggle for racial equality.

Because it suggests the specific direction your research will take as well as the scope and emphasis of your argument, the tentative thesis you come up with at this point can help you generate a list of the main ideas you plan to develop in your paper. This list of points can help you to narrow the focus of your research so that you can zero in on a few specific categories to explore as you read and take notes.

Tentative Thesis: Buffalo Soldiers were pioneers in the struggle for racial equality.

- Give background about westward expansion during the mid-nineteenth century.
- Identify need for military presence.
- Explain how the Buffalo Soldiers were created.
- Discuss the challenges they faced.
- Discuss their accomplishments.

27e Doing Focused Research

Once you have decided on a tentative thesis and made a list of the points you plan to discuss in your paper, you are ready to begin your focused research. When you do **focused research,** you look for the specific information—facts, examples, statistics, definitions, quotations—you need to support your points.

(1) Reading Sources

As you look for information, try to explore as many sources, and as many different viewpoints, as possible. It makes sense to examine more sources than you actually intend to use. This strategy will enable you to proceed even if one or more of your sources turns out to be biased, outdated, unreliable, superficial, or irrelevant—in other words, unusable. Exploring different viewpoints is just as important. After all, if you read only those sources that agree on a particular issue, it will be difficult for you to develop a viewpoint of your own.

As you explore various sources, try not to waste time reading irrelevant material; instead, try to evaluate each source's potential usefulness to you as quickly as possible. For example, if your source is a book, skim the table of contents and the index; if your source is a journal article, read the abstract. Then, if an article or a section of a book seems potentially useful, photocopy it for future reference. Similarly, when you find an online source that looks promising, resist the temptation to paste it directly into a section of your paper-in-progress. Instead, print it out (or send it to yourself as an e-mail) so that you can evaluate it further later on. (For information on evaluating library sources, see **28b;** for information on evaluating Internet sources, see **29c.**)

(2) Balancing Primary and Secondary Sources

In the course of your focused research, you will encounter both **primary sources** (original documents and observations) and **secondary sources** (interpretations of original documents and observations).

PRIMARY AND SECONDARY SOURCES

Primary Source	Secondary Source
Novel, poem, play, film	Criticism
Diary, autobiography	Biography
Letter, historical document, speech, oral history	Historical analysis
Newspaper article	Editorial
Raw data from questionnaires or interviews	Social science article; case study
Observation/experiment	Scientific article

Primary sources are essential for many research projects, but secondary sources, which provide scholars' insights and interpretations, are also valuable. Remember, though, that the farther you get from the primary source, the more chances exist for inaccuracies introduced by researchers' inadvertent misinterpretations or distortions.

27f Taking Notes

As you locate information in the library and on the Internet, you take notes to keep a record of exactly what you found and where you found it. Each piece of information that you record in your notes (whether summarized, paraphrased, or quoted from your sources) should be accompanied by a short descriptive heading that indicates its relevance to one of the points you will develop in your paper. Also include a brief comment that makes clear your reasons for recording the information and identifies what you think it will contribute to your paper. This comment (enclosed in brackets so you will know it expresses your own ideas, not those of your source) should establish the purpose of your note—what you think it can explain, support, clarify, describe, or contradict—and perhaps suggest its relationship to other notes or other sources. Any questions you have about the information or its source can also be included in your comment. Finally, each note should fully and accurately identify the source of the information you are recording.

(1) Managing Source Information

When you take notes, your goal is flexibility: you want to be able to arrange and rearrange information easily and efficiently as your paper takes shape. If you take notes on your computer, type each piece of information under a specific heading on a separate page; don't list all information from a single source under one general heading. If you take notes by hand, you may decide to use the time-honored index card system. If you do, write on only one side of the card, and be sure to use a separate index card for each piece of information rather than running several ideas together on a single card. (See Figures 3 and 4.)

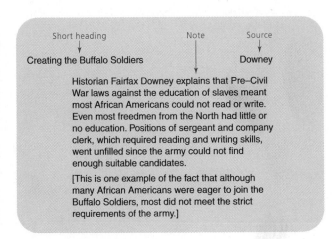

Short heading   Note   Source

Creating the Buffalo Soldiers   Downey

Historian Fairfax Downey explains that Pre–Civil War laws against the education of slaves meant most African Americans could not read or write. Even most freedmen from the North had little or no education. Positions of sergeant and company clerk, which required reading and writing skills, went unfilled since the army could not find enough suitable candidates.

[This is one example of the fact that although many African Americans were eager to join the Buffalo Soldiers, most did not meet the strict requirements of the army.]

Figure 3 Note (in computer file)

Source

Short heading →

Note (summary, paraphrase, or quotation) →

Your comments (opinions, reactions, purpose of → note, connections with other sources, etc.)

> Racism in the military   Cooke
>
> Cooke writes that a typical notice from the Army and Navy Journal reads: "A first Lieutenant of Infantry (white) stationed at a very desirable post desires a transfer with an officer of the same grade, on equal terms if in a white regiment; but if in a colored regiment, a reasonable bonus would be expected."
>
> [This exemplifies the kind of racism African Americans faced in the military.]

Figure 4 Note (on index card)

✔ CHECKLIST: TAKING NOTES

✔ **Identify the source of each piece of information clearly and completely**—even if the source is sitting on your bookshelf or stored in your computer's hard drive.

✔ **Include everything now that you will need later** to understand your note—names, dates, places, connections with other notes—and to remember why you recorded it.

✔ **Distinguish quotations from paraphrases and summaries and your own ideas from those of your sources.** If you copy a source's words, place them in quotation marks. (If you take notes by hand, circle the quotation marks; if you type your notes, boldface the quotation marks.) If you write down your own ideas, bracket them and, if you are typing, italicize them as well. (Using these techniques will help you avoid **plagiarism** in your paper.)

✔ **Copy each author's comments accurately,** using the exact words, spelling, punctuation marks, and capitalization.

✔ **Put an author's comments into your own words whenever possible,** summarizing and paraphrasing material as well as adding your own observations and analysis.

See
Ch.
30

PHOTOCOPIES AND COMPUTER PRINTOUTS

Making photocopies and printing out sections of electronic sources that you have downloaded can be useful, time-saving strategies, but photocopies and computer printouts are no substitute for notes. In fact, copying information is only the first step in the process of taking thorough, careful notes on a source. You should be especially careful not to allow the ease and efficiency of copying to encourage you to postpone decisions about the usefulness of your information. Remember, you can easily accumulate so many pages that it will be almost impossible to keep track of all your information.

Also keep in mind that photocopies and printouts do not have the flexibility of notes you take yourself because a single page of text may include information that should be earmarked for several different sections of your paper. This lack of flexibility makes it difficult for you to arrange source material into any meaningful order.

Finally, remember that the annotations you make on photocopies and printouts are usually not focused or polished enough to be incorporated directly into your paper. You will still have to paraphrase and summarize your source's ideas and make connections among them. Therefore, you should approach a photocopy or printout just as you approach any other print source—as material that you will read, highlight, annotate, and then take notes about.

✔ CHECKLIST: WORKING WITH PHOTOCOPIES AND COMPUTER PRINTOUTS

- ✔ Record full and accurate source information, including the inclusive page numbers, electronic address (URL), and any other relevant information, on the first page of each copy.
- ✔ Clip or staple together consecutive pages of a single source.

continued on the following page

continued from the previous page

✔ Do not copy a source without reminding yourself—*in writing*—why you are doing so. In pencil or on removable self-stick notes, record your initial responses to the source's ideas, jot down cross references to other works or notes, and highlight important sections.

✔ Photocopying can be time-consuming and expensive, so try to avoid copying material that is only marginally relevant to your paper.

✔ Keep photocopies and printouts in a file so you will be able to find them when you need them.

(2) Summarizing, Paraphrasing, and Quoting

Summarizing Sources   A **summary** is a brief restatement in your own words of a source's main idea. When you summarize a source, you condense the author's ideas into a few concise sentences. You do *not* include your own opinions or interpretations of the writer's ideas.

Original Source

By the end of the war nearly 180,000 Negroes had served in the Union army and taps had sounded over the bodies of 33,380 of them who had given their lives for freedom and Union. Despite their record there were many who still doubted that the Negro could be a first-rate combat soldier, and his future in the Army of the United States remained clouded in uncertainty.

On May 23–24, 1865, the Union army staged its last great spectacle. Nearly a quarter of a million men passed in grand review along Pennsylvania Avenue in the nation's capital. Swiftly then, the United States reverted to its traditional policy of a small peacetime army. Within little more than a year the military establishment had been all but dismantled and the authorized strength of the army was only 54,641 men—the actual strength was considerably less. This was the situation in the face of a savage Indian war in the West and conditions approaching anarchy along the Mexican border.

Congress, meanwhile, had cleared up some of the uncertainty surrounding the future of the Negro in the armed forces, and, in doing so, altered the face of military tradition. By an act passed on July 28, 1866, provisions were made for the Negro to serve in the regular peacetime army. (William Leckie, *The Buffalo Soldiers: A Narrative of Negro Cavalry in the West* [Norman: University of Oklahoma Press, 1975]).

Summary   As Leckie observes, after the Civil War, a large Union army was no longer needed. As the United States transitioned to a small peacetime army, the future of African Americans who had served during the Civil War was uncertain. Recognizing that African Americans had proved their abilities as soldiers during the Civil War, Congress passed an act in 1866 that allowed them to serve in the peacetime army.[1]

✔ CHECKLIST: SUMMARIZING A SOURCE

✔ Reread your source until you understand its main idea.
✔ Write your summary, using your own words and phrasing. If you quote a distinctive word or phrase, use quotation marks.
✔ Add appropriate documentation.

Paraphrasing Sources   A summary conveys just the essence of a source; a **paraphrase** is a *detailed* restatement, in your own words, of all a source's important ideas—but not your opinions or interpretations of those ideas. In a paraphrase, you indicate not only the source's main points but also its order, tone, and emphasis. Consequently, a paraphrase can sometimes be as long as the source itself.

Compare the following paraphrase with the summary of the same source above.

Paraphrase

With the Civil War over, maintaining a large Union army was no longer practical. From a high of almost a quarter of a million, the army reduced its strength to just over fifty six thousand.[1] However, the postwar army would have to take charge of security in the South during Reconstruction as well as maintain order along the frontier and guard the U.S.–Mexican border. As Leckie explains, even though their numbers may have been drastically reduced, their responsibilities were not. As Civil War soldiers returned to civilian life, new recruits were needed. As a result, the first peacetime regiments of African Americans were formed.

✔ CHECKLIST: PARAPHRASING A SOURCE

- ✔ Reread your source until you understand its key points.
- ✔ List the key points in the order in which they appear in the source.
- ✔ Write your paraphrase, following the order, tone, and emphasis of the original. Use your own words and phrasing; if you quote a distinctive word or phrase, use quotation marks.
- ✔ Add appropriate documentation.

SUMMARIZING AND PARAPHRASING SOURCES

When you summarize or paraphrase, be sure to familiarize yourself with your source before you begin to write, and then try not to look at it again until you are finished. Use language and syntax that come naturally to you, and be careful not to duplicate the wording or sentence structure of the source. If you cannot think of a synonym for an important word or phrase that appears in the source, place it in quotation marks.

Quoting Sources   When you **quote,** you copy an author's remarks exactly as they appear in a source, word for word and punctuation mark for punctuation mark, enclosing the borrowed words in quotation marks. As a rule, you should not quote extensively in a research paper. The use of numerous quotations interrupts the flow of your discussion and gives readers the impression that your paper is just an unassimilated collection of other people's ideas.

WHEN TO QUOTE

- Quote when a source's wording or phrasing is so distinctive that a summary or paraphrase would diminish its impact.
- Quote when a source's words—particularly those of a recognized expert on your subject—will lend authority to your paper.

continued on the following page

continued from the previous page

- Quote when paraphrasing would create a long, clumsy, or incoherent phrase or would change the meaning of the original.
- Quote when you plan to disagree with a source. Using a source's exact words helps to assure readers that you are being fair.

27g Deciding on a Thesis

After you have finished your focused research and note taking, you must refine your tentative thesis into a carefully worded statement that expresses a conclusion that your research can support. This **thesis statement** should be more detailed than your tentative thesis, accurately conveying the direction, emphasis, and scope of your paper.

See 1b

DECIDING ON A THESIS

Tentative Thesis
Buffalo Soldiers were pioneers in the struggle for racial equality.

Thesis Statement
In spite of harsh treatment, the Buffalo Soldiers served their country and acted as pioneers not only in the American West but also in the struggle for racial equality.

27h Outlining, Drafting, and Revising

Keeping your thesis in mind, you are now ready to outline your supporting points and draft your paper.

(1) Outlining

Before you write your rough draft, you should make an outline. At this point, you need to make some sense out of all the notes you have accumulated, and you do this by sorting and organizing them. By identifying categories and subcategories of information, you begin to see your paper take shape and are able to construct an outline that reflects this shape. A **formal outline** indicates not only the exact order in which you will present your ideas but also the relationship between main ideas and supporting details.

NOTE: The outline you construct at this stage is only a g... for you to follow as you draft your paper; it is likely to change. you draft and revise. The final outline, written after your pap... is complete, will reflect what you have written and serve as a guide for your readers.

✔ CHECKLIST: PREPARING A FORMAL OUTLINE

- ✔ Write your thesis statement at the top of the page.
- ✔ Review your notes to make sure that each note expresses only one general idea. If this is not the case, recopy any unrelated information, creating a separate note.
- ✔ Check that the heading for each note specifically characterizes the note's information. If it does not, change the heading.
- ✔ Sort your notes by their headings, keeping a miscellaneous pile for notes that do not seem to fit into any category. Irrelevant notes—those unrelated to your paper's thesis—should be set aside (but not discarded).
- ✔ Check your categories for balance. If most of your notes fall into one or two categories, rewrite some of your headings to create narrower, more focused categories. If you have only one or two notes in a category, you will need to do additional research or treat that topic only briefly (or not at all).
- ✔ Organize the individual notes within each group, adding more specific subheads as needed. Arrange your notes in an order that highlights the most important points and subordinates lesser ones.
- ✔ Decide on a logical order in which to discuss your paper's major points.
- ✔ Construct your formal outline, using divisions and subdivisions that correspond to your headings. (Outline only the body of your paper, not your introduction and conclusion.) Be sure each heading has at least two subheadings; if one does not, combine it with another heading. Follow outline format strictly.

continued on the following page

continued from the previous page

    I. First major point of your paper
        A. First subpoint
        B. Next subpoint
            1. First supporting example
            2. Next supporting example
                a. First specific detail
                b. Next specific detail
    II. Second major point

✔ Review your completed outline to make sure you
   have not placed too much emphasis on a relatively
   unimportant idea, ordered ideas illogically, or created
   sections that overlap with others.

OUTLINING

Before you begin writing, create a separate file for
each major section of your outline. Then, copy your
notes into these files in the order in which you intend to
use them. You can print out each file as you need it and
use it for a guide as you write.

(2) Drafting

When you are ready to write your **rough draft**, arrange your ^{See} ^{1d1}
notes in the order in which you intend to use them. Follow your
outline as you write, using your notes as needed. As you draft,
jot down questions to yourself, and identify points that need
further clarification (you can bracket those ideas or print them
in boldface on a typed draft, or you can write them on self-stick
notes). Leave space for material you plan to add, and bracket
phrases or whole sections that you think you may later decide to
move or delete. In other words, lay the groundwork for a major
revision. Remember that even though you are guided by an outline and notes, you are not bound to follow their content or sequence exactly. As you write, new ideas or new connections
among ideas may occur to you. If you find yourself wandering
from your thesis or outline, check to see whether the departure
is justified.

As your draft takes shape, you will probably find that each paragraph corresponds to one major point on your outline. Be sure to supply transitions between sentences and paragraphs to show how your points are related. To make it easy for you to revise later on, triple-space your draft. Be careful to copy source information fully and accurately on this and every subsequent draft, placing the documentation as close as possible to the material it identifies.

DRAFTING

You can use a split screen or multiple windows to view your notes as you draft your paper. You can also copy the material that you need from your notes and then insert it into the text of your paper. (As you copy, be especially careful that you do not unintentionally commit **plagiarism**).

See
30b

Shaping the Parts of Your Paper   Like any other essay, a research paper has an introduction, a body, and a conclusion. In your rough draft, as in your outline, you focus on the body of your paper. You should not spend time planning an introduction or a conclusion at this stage; your ideas will change as you write, and you will want to revise your opening and closing paragraphs later to reflect those changes.

In your **introduction,** you identify your topic and establish how you will approach it. Your **introduction** also includes your thesis statement, which expresses the position you will support in the rest of the paper. Sometimes the introductory paragraphs briefly summarize your major supporting points (the major divisions of your outline) in the order in which you will present them. Such a preview of your thesis and support provides a smooth transition into the body of your paper. Your introduction can also present an overview of the problem you will discuss, or it can summarize research already done on your topic. In your rough draft, however, an undeveloped introduction is perfectly acceptable; in fact, your thesis statement alone can serve as a placeholder for the more polished introduction that you will write later.

See
2d

As you draft the **body** of your paper, indicate its direction with strong **topic sentences** that correspond to the divisions of your outline.

See
2a

> Those serving in the Buffalo Soldiers rarely received praise or promotions from high command because of the racism infecting the army, but the officers who served with them came to respect them as soldiers and as men.

You can also use <u>**subheadings**</u> to organize content and to See 34a guide readers through your paper.

Westward Expansion and the American Military

As Michael T. Lubbrage explains, with the end of the

Civil War, "Go West young man" became America's

unofficial motto.

Even in your rough draft, carefully worded headings and topic sentences will help you keep your discussion under control.

The **conclusion** of a research paper often restates the thesis. This is especially important in a long paper, because by the time your readers get to the end, they may have lost sight of your paper's main idea. Your <u>**conclusion**</u> can also include a sum- See 2d mary of your key points, a call for action, or perhaps an apt quotation. In your rough draft, however, your concluding paragraph is usually very brief.

Working Source Material into Your Paper   In the body of your paper, you evaluate and interpret your sources, comparing different ideas and assessing conflicting points of view. As a writer, your job is to draw your own conclusions, blending information from various sources into a paper that coherently and forcefully presents your own original viewpoint to your readers.

Your source material must be smoothly integrated into your paper, and the relationships among various sources (and between those sources' ideas and your own) must be clearly and accurately identified. If two sources present conflicting interpretations, you must be especially careful to use precise language and accurate transitions to make the contrast apparent ,for instance,

Like William Katz, historian Sara Massey remarks

that the Buffalo Soldiers kept the peace by subduing

Indian raiding parties. She adds that they also helped map

and settle large portions of the frontier.

When two sources agree, you should make this clear (for example, "Lubbrage and many other historians argue that . . ."). Such phrasing will provide a context for your own comments and conclusions. If different sources present complementary information about a subject, blend details from the sources *carefully,* keeping track of which details come from which source.

(3) Revising

A good way to start revising is to check to see that your thesis statement still accurately expresses your paper's central focus. Then, make an outline of your draft, and compare it with the outline you made before you began the draft. If you find significant differences, you will have to revise your thesis statement or rewrite sections of your paper. The checklists in **1d2** can guide your revision of your paper's overall structure and its individual paragraphs, sentences, and words.

✔ CHECKLIST: REVISING A RESEARCH PAPER

✔ Should you do more research to find support for certain points?

✔ Do you need to reorder the major sections of your paper?

✔ Should you rearrange the order in which you present your points within those sections?

✔ Do you need to add section headings? transitional paragraphs?

See 30a
✔ Have you **integrated your notes** smoothly into your paper?

See 30a1
✔ Do you introduce source material with **identifying tags**?

✔ Are quotations blended with paraphrase, summary, and your own observations and reactions?

See 30b
✔ Have you avoided **plagiarism** by carefully documenting all borrowed ideas?

✔ Have you analyzed and interpreted the ideas of others rather than simply stringing those ideas together?

✔ Do your own ideas—not those of your sources—dominate your discussion?

 REVISING

When you finish revising your paper, copy the file that contains your working bibliography, title it "Bibliography," and insert it at the end of your paper. (Make sure that the format of the entries on your bibliography conforms to the Chicago documentation style.)

PREPARING A FINAL DRAFT

Before you print out the final version of your paper, **edit and proofread** not just the paper itself but also your outline and your bibliography list. Next, consider (or reconsider) your paper's **title.** It should be descriptive enough to tell your readers what your paper is about, and it should create interest in your subject. Your title should also be consistent with the purpose and tone of your paper. (You would hardly want a humorous title for a paper about the death penalty or world hunger.) Finally, your title should be engaging and to the point—and perhaps even provocative. Often a quotation from one of your sources will suggest a likely title.

See 1e

When you are satisfied with your title, read your paper through one last time, proofreading for any grammar, spelling, or typing errors you may have missed. Pay particular attention to parenthetical documentation and in your bibliography entries. (Remember that every error undermines your credibility.) Finally, make sure your paper's format conforms to your instructor's guidelines. Once you are satisfied that your paper is as accurate as you can make it, print it out. Then, fasten the pages with a paper clip (do not staple the pages or fold the corners together), and hand it in.

CHAPTER 28

USING AND EVALUATING LIBRARY SOURCES

28a Using Library Sources

Even though the Internet has changed the nature of research, the library is still the best place to begin a research project. With its wide variety of print and electronic resources—some suitable for **exploratory research**, others for **focused research**—the library gives you access to material that you cannot get anywhere else.

See 27b
See 27e

(1) Using the Online Catalog

Most college and other libraries have abandoned print catalog systems in favor of **online catalogs**—computer databases that list all the books, journals, and other materials held by the library.

You access the online catalog (as well as the other electronic resources of the library) by using computer terminals located throughout the library. Typing in certain words or phrases—*search terms*—enables you to find the information you need. When you search an online catalog for information about a topic, you can conduct either a *keyword search* or a *subject search.*

Conducting a Keyword Search   When you carry out a keyword search, you enter into the online catalog a term or terms associated with your topic. The computer then retrieves catalog entries that contain those words. The more precise your search terms, the more specific and useful the information you will receive. (Combining search terms with AND, OR, and NOT enables you to narrow or broaden your search. This technique is called conducting a **Boolean search**.)

See 29a2

Conducting a Subject Search   When you carry out a subject search, you enter specific subject headings into the online catalog. The subject headings in the library are most often arranged according to headings listed in the five-volume manual *Library of Congress Subject Headings,* which is held at the reference desk of your library. Although it may be possible to guess at a subject heading, your search will be more successful if you consult these volumes to identify the exact words you need.

(2) Using Electronic Resources

Today's college libraries have electronic resources that enable you to find a wide variety of sources. Many of the print sources located in the library are also available in electronic format. For example, **periodical indexes** such as *Readers' Guide to Periodical Literature* and *Expanded Academic ASAP* offer bibliographic citations, abstracts, and full articles in journals, magazines, and newspapers. Other online databases enable you to access general reference works, such as encyclopedias and bibliographies, as well as indexes on specific topics of interest to historians, such as *American Historical Review* and *Foreign Affairs 50-Year Index.* Often, the same computer terminals that enable you to access the online catalog also allow you to access online databases. Information stored on CD-ROM and DVD is accessed on computers located in the reference section of the library. See 28a6

NOTE: In general, the electronic resources of the library enable you to access more specialized databases than you can access on the Internet. For this reason, be sure to use these resources whenever you are assigned a research project.

(3) Consulting General Reference Works

During your exploratory research, general reference works can provide a broad overview of a particular subject. The following reference works, available in electronic form as well as in print, are useful for exploratory research.

General Encyclopedias   General multivolume encyclopedias are available both in electronic format and in print. For example, *The New Encyclopaedia Britannica* is available on CD-ROM and DVD, as well as on the World Wide Web at (http://www.britannica.com).

Specialized Encyclopedias, Dictionaries, and Bibliographies These specialized reference works contain in-depth articles focusing on a single subject area.

General Bibliographies   General bibliographies list books available in a wide variety of fields.

> *Books in Print.* An index of authors and titles of books in print in the United States. The *Subject Guide to Books in Print* indexes books according to subject area.
>
> *The Bibliographic Index.* A tool for locating bibliographies.

Biographical References   Biographical reference books provide information about people's lives as well as bibliographic listings.

Living Persons

Who's Who in America. Concise biographical information about prominent Americans.

Who's Who. Collection of concise biographical facts about notable British men and women.

Current Biography. Biography that includes articles on people of many nationalities.

Deceased Persons

Dictionary of American Biography. Considered the best of American biographical dictionaries. Includes articles on over 13,000 Americans.

Dictionary of National Biography. The most important reference work for British biography.

Webster's Biographical Dictionary. Perhaps the most widely used biographical reference work. Includes people from all periods and places.

(4) Consulting Specialized Reference Works

More specialized reference works can help you find facts, examples, statistics, definitions, and quotations. The following reference works—many of which are available on CD-ROM, on DVD, or online as well as in print versions—are most useful for focused research.

Unabridged Dictionaries Unabridged dictionaries, such as the *Oxford English Dictionary,* are comprehensive works that give detailed information about words.

Historical Dictionaries Historical dictionaries, such as *Concise Dictionary of American History,* define historical terms and provide information about each term's origin and historical context.

Special Dictionaries These dictionaries focus on such topics as usage, synonyms, slang and idioms, etymologies, and foreign terms; some focus on specific disciplines, such as accounting or law.

Historical Encyclopedias Historical encyclopedias such as *The Encyclopedia of the Middle Ages* and *Encyclopedia of World History* provide detailed information about different time periods and places.

Yearbooks and Almanacs A **yearbook** is an annual publication that updates factual and statistical information already published in a reference source. An **almanac** provides lists, charts, and statistics about a wide variety of subjects.

World Almanac. Almanac that includes statistics about government, population, sports, and many other subjects. Published annually since 1868.

Information Please Almanac. Almanac that includes information unavailable in the *World Almanac.* Published annually since 1947.

Facts on File. Covering 1940 to the present, this work offers digests of important news stories from metropolitan newspapers.

Editorials on File. Reprints of important editorials from American and Canadian newspapers.

Atlases An **atlas** contains maps and charts as well as historical, cultural, political, and economic information.

National Geographic Society. *National Geographic Atlas of the World.* The most up-to-date atlas available.

Rand McNally Cosmopolitan World Atlas. A modern and extremely legible medium-sized atlas.

We the People: An Atlas of America's Ethnic Diversity. Presentation of information about specific ethnic groups. Maps show immigration routes and settlement patterns.

Historical Atlases Historical atlases, such as *Muir's Historical Atlas: Ancient, Medieval & Modern,* include maps, charts, and historical information.

Biographical Collections Biographical collections provide short biographies of well-known persons and focus on accomplishments by individuals. They include *Who's Who, American National Biography, and Research Guide to American Historical Biography.*

Quotation Books A **quotation book** contains numerous quotations on a wide variety of subjects. Such quotations can be especially useful for your paper's introductory and concluding paragraphs.

Bartlett's Familiar quotations. Quotations are arranged chronologically by author.

The Home Book of Quotations. Quotations are arranged by subject. An author index and a keyword index are also included.

(5) Finding Books

The online catalog gives you the call numbers you need for locating specific titles. A **call number** is like a book's address in the library: it tells you exactly where to find the book you are looking for.

AUTHOR: Davis, William C.
TITLE: Battle at Bull Run: a history of the first major campaign
    of the Civil War
EDITION: 1st ed.
CALL NUMBER: E 472.18.D 39
PUBLISHED: Garden City, NY: Doubleday 1977.
DESCRIPTION: xxiii, 298p.: [8] leaves of plates : ill.; 22 cm.
NOTES: Includes index.
      Bibliography: p. [279]-287.
SUBJECTS: Bull Run, 1st Battle of, Va, 1861.
OTHER AUTHORS: Davis, William C.
ISBN: 0385122616 :
OCLC Number: 02985792

Figure 1 Online Catalog Entry

(6) Finding Articles

A **periodical** is a newspaper, magazine, scholarly journal, or other publication that is published at regular intervals (weekly, monthly, or quarterly). **Periodical indexes** list articles from a selected group of magazines, newspapers, or scholarly journals. These indexes may be available in your library in bound volumes, on microfilm or microfiche, on CD-ROM or DVD, or online. Choosing the right index for your research saves you time and energy by allowing you to easily find articles written about your subject.

NOTE: Articles in scholarly journals provide current information and are written by experts in the field. Because these journals focus on a particular subject area, they can provide in-depth analysis.

PERIODICAL INDEXES AND GUIDES FOR HISTORY

*Historical Periodicals: An Annotated World List of
    Historical and Related Serial Publications
Historical Periodicals Directory*

continued on the following page

continued from the previous page

Historical Abstracts
America: History and Life: A Guide to Periodical Literature
Guide to American Historical Review, 1894–1945
Women's Magazines, 1693–1968
Reader's Guide to Periodical Literature
Nineteenth-Century Reader's Guide to Periodical
    Literature
Public Affairs Information Service Bulletin
The Combined Retrospective Index Set to Journals
    in History
Social Science and Humanities Index
Poole's Index to Periodical Literature
Social Sciences Index
Humanities Index

SPECIALIZED PERIODICAL INDEXES FOR RESEARCH ON HISTORICAL EVENTS

Agricultural Index
Applied Science and Technology Index
Art Index
Business Periodicals Index
Education Index
Index to Legal Periodicals
Index Medicus
Music Index
American Historical Review, General Index for Volumes
    41–70, 1935–1965
Guide to the American Historical Review, 1895–1945
Women's Magazines, 1693–1968
Hispanic American Periodicals Index
Foreign Affairs 50-Year Index: Vols. 1–50, 1922–1972
The Pacific Historical Review: A Cumulative Index to
    Volumes 1–43, 1932–1974
Fifty Year Index: Mississippi Valley Historical Review,
    1914–1964
Index to Economic Journals
Guide to the Hispanic American Historical Review:
    1918–1945, 1945–1955
Index to the Canadian Historical Review

WELL-KNOWN HISTORICAL PERIODICALS

Agricultural History
American Historical Review
American Jewish History
The American Journal of Legal History
American Quarterly
The Americas
Bulletin of the Institute of Historical Research
Business History Review
Cambridge Historical Journal
Canadian Journal of History
Central European History
China Quarterly
Comparative Studies in Society and History
Current History
Daedalus
Diplomatic History
Early Medieval History
Economic History Review
Economic Journal
Eighteenth Century Studies
English Historical Review
Ethnohistory
Feminist Studies
Film and History
French Historical Studies
Gender and History
Hispanic American Historical Review
The Historian
Historical Journal
Historical Methods
Historical Research
History
History and Theory
History of Education Quarterly
History of Political Economy
History of Religions
The History Teacher
International Journal of African Historical Studies
International Review of Social History
Irish Historical Studies
Isis
Journal of African History

continued on the following page

continued from the previous page

Journal of American History
Journal of American Studies
Journal of Asian Studies
Journal of Black Studies
Journal of British Studies
Journal of Canadian Studies
Journal of Contemporary History
Journal of Early Republic
Journal of Ecclesiastical History

NOTE: Not all libraries will provide access to these indexes from outside the library.

Microfilm and Microfiche   Extremely small images of pages of a periodical may be stored on microfilm. (You need a microfilm scanner to read or photocopy the pages.) Microfiche is similar to microfilm, but images are on a 5-by-7-inch sheet of film and are scanned with a microfiche reader.

(7) Using Special Library Services

As you do focused research, consult a librarian if you plan to use any of the following special services.

SPECIAL LIBRARY SERVICES

- **Interlibrary Loans**   Your library may be part of a library system that allows loans of books from one location to another. Check with your librarian.
- **Special Collections**   Your library may house special collections of books, manuscripts, or documents.
- **Government Documents**   A large university library may have a separate government documents area with its own catalog or index.
- **Vertical File**   The vertical file includes pamphlets from a variety of organizations and interest groups, newspaper clippings, and other material collected by librarians.

28b   Evaluating Library Sources

Whenever you find information in the library (print or electronic), you should take the time to **evaluate** it—to assess its usefulness and its reliability. To determine the usefulness of a library source, you should ask yourself the following questions.

Does the Source Treat Your Topic in Enough Detail? To be useful, your source should treat your topic in detail. Skim the book's table of contents and index for references to your topic. To be of any real help, a book should include a section or chapter on your topic, not simply a footnote of brief reference. For articles, read the abstract, or skim the entire article for key facts, looking closely at section headings, information set in boldface type, and topic sentences. An article should have your topic as its central subject, or at least one of its main concerns.

Is the Source Current? The date of publication tells you whether the information in a book or article is up-to-date. A source's currency is particularly important for scientific and technological subjects. Beu even in the humanities, new discoveries and new ways of thinking lead scholars to reevaluate and modify their ideas. Be sure to check with your instructor to see if he or she prefers sources that have been published after a particular date.

Is the Source Respected? A contemporary review of a source can help you make this assessment. *Book Review Digest,* available in the reference section of your library, lists popular books that have been reviewed in at least three newspapers or magazines and includes excerpts from representative reviews. Book reviews are also available from the *New York Times Book Review's* Web site (http://www.nytimes.com/books), which includes text of book reviews the newspaper has published since 1980.

Is the Source Reliable? Is a piece of writing largely fact or unsubstantiated opinion? Does the author support his or her conclusions? Does the author include documentation? Is the supporting information balanced? Is the author objective, or does he or she have a particular agenda to advance? Is the author associated with a special interest group that may affect his or her view of the issue?

In general, **scholarly publications**—books and journals aimed at an audience of expert readers—are more respected and reliable than **popular publications**—books, magazines, and newspapers aimed at an audience of general readers. Assuming they are current and written by reputable authors, however, articles from popular publications may be appropriate for your research. But remember that not all popular publications adhere to the same rigorous standards as scholarly publications. For example, although some popular periodicals (such as *Atlantic Monthly* and *Harper's*) generally contain articles that are reliable and carefully researched, other periodicals do not. For this reason, before you use information from popular sources such as *Newsweek* or *Sports Illustrated,* check with your instructor.

The following box summarizes the differences between scholarly and popular publications.

SCHOLARLY AND POPULAR PUBLICATIONS

Scholarly Publications	Popular Publications
Scholarly publications report the results of research.	Popular publications entertain and inform.
Scholarly publications are frequently published by a university press or have some connection with a university or academic organization.	Popular publications are published by commercial presses.
Scholarly publications are **refereed;** that is, an editorial board or group of expert reviewers determines what will be published.	Popular publications are usually not refereed.
Scholarly publications are usually written by someone who is a recognized authority in the field about which he or she is writing.	Popular publications may be written by experts in a particular field, but more often they are written by staff or freelance writers.
Scholarly publications are written for a scholarly audience, so they often contain a highly technical vocabulary and challenging content.	Popular publications are written for general readers, so they usually use accessible language and do not have very challenging content.
Scholarly publications nearly always contain extensive documentation as well as a bibliography of works consulted.	Popular publications rarely cite sources or use documentation.
Scholarly publications are published primarily because they make a contribution to a particular field of study.	Popular publications are published primarily to make a profit.

CHAPTER 29

USING AND EVALUATING
INTERNET SOURCES

The **Internet** is a vast system of networks that links millions of computers. Because of its size and diversity, the Internet allows people from all over the world to communicate quickly and easily.

Furthermore, because it is inexpensive to publish text, pictures, and sound online (via the Internet), businesses, government agencies, libraries, and universities are able to make available vast amounts of information: years' worth of newspaper articles, hundreds of thousands of pages of scientific or technical papers, government reports, images of all the paintings in a museum, virtual tours of historically significant buildings or sites—even an entire library of literature.

29a Using the World Wide Web for Research

When most people refer to the Internet, they actually mean the **World Wide Web,** which is just a part of the Internet. (See **29b** for other components of the Internet that you can use in your research.) The Web relies on **hypertext links,** connections between Web pages that appear as icons or as highlighted or underlined text. By clicking your mouse on one of these links, you can move easily from one part of a document to another or from one Web site to another. The Web has become a powerful tool that can give you access to a great deal of print information as well as graphics, sound, animation, film clips, and even live video.

The Web enables you to connect to a vast variety of documents. For example, you can call up a **home page** or **Web page** (an individual document), or a **Web site** (a collection of Web pages). Government agencies, businesses, universities, libraries, newspapers and magazines, journals, and public interest groups, as well as individuals, all operate their own Web sites. Each of these sites contains hypertext links that can take you to other relevant sites. By using these links, you can "surf the Net," following your interests and moving from one document to another.

To carry out a Web search, you need a **Web browser,** a tool that enables you to find information on the Web. Two of the most popular browsers—*Netscape Navigator* and *Microsoft Internet Explorer*—display the full range of text, photos, sound, and video available in Web documents. Most new computers come with one of these browsers already installed.

Before you can access the Web, you have to be **online,** connected to an Internet service provider (ISP). Most colleges and universities provide Internet access to students free of charge. Once you are online, you have to use your browser to connect to a **search engine,** a program that helps you retrieve information by searching the documents that are available on the Internet.

 MOST POPULAR SEARCH ENGINES

AltaVista (www.altavista.com): Good engine for precise searches. Fast and easy to use.

Ask Jeeves (www.askjeeves.com): Good beginner's site. Allows you to narrow your search by asking questions, such as *Are dogs smarter than pigs?*

Excite (www.excite.com): Good for general topics. Because it searches over 250 million Web sites, you often get more information than you need.

Google (www.google.com): Excellent, fast, thorough search engine. Currently, the most popular search engine.

Hotbot (www.hotbot.com): Excellent, fast search engine for locating specific information. Good search options allow you to fine-tune your searches.

Infoseek (www.infoseek.com): Enables you to access information in a directory of reviewed sites, news stories, and Usenet groups.

Lycos (www.lycos.com): Enables you to search for specific media (graphics, for example). A somewhat small index of Web pages.

Northern Light (www.northernlight.com): Searches Web pages but also lists pay-for-view articles not always listed by other search engines. Arranges results under subject headings.

WebCrawler (www.webcrawler.com): Good for beginners. Easy to use and very forgiving.

Yahoo! (www.yahoo.com): Enables you to search using both subject headings and keywords. Searches its own indexes as well as the Web.

SPECIALIZED SEARCH ENGINES

Bizbot (business search engine)
http://www.bizbot.net/

FedWorld (U.S. government database and report search engine)
http://www.fedworld.gov/

FindLaw (legal search engine)
http://www.findlaw.com/

HealthFinder (health, nutrition, and disease information for consumers)
http://www.heathfinder.gov/

The Internet Movie Database (search engine and database for film facts, reviews, and so on)
http://www.imdb.com

Newsbot (news search engine)
http://www.lycos.com/news/

Pilot-Search.com (literary search engine)
http://www.Pilot-Search.com/

SportQuest (sports search engine)
http://www.sportquest.com/

Voice of the Shuttle (humanities search engine)
http://www.vos.ucsb.edu/

Because even the best search engines search only a fraction of what is on the Web, you should also carry out a metasearch using a **metacrawler,** a search engine that searches several search engines simultaneously. Dogpile (www.dogpile.com), Google (www.google.com), and Metacrawler (www.metacrawler.com) are useful tools for finding out the full range of online sources that are available.

There are three ways to use search engines to find the information you want.

(1) Entering an Electronic Address

The most basic way to access information on the Web is to go directly to a specific electronic address. Search engines and Web browsers display a box that enables you to enter the electronic address (URL) of a specific Web site. Once you type in an address and click on *search* (or hit *enter* or the return key), you will be connected to the Web site you want. Make sure that you type the electronic address exactly as it appears, without adding spaces or adding or deleting punctuation marks. Remember that omitting just a single letter or punctuation mark will send you to the wrong site—or to no site at all.

(2) Doing a Keyword Search

Search engines also enable you to do a keyword search. On the first page of the search engine that you have chosen, you will find a box in which you can enter a keyword (or keywords). When you hit *enter* or the return key, the search engine retrieves and displays all the Web pages that contain your keywords.

Keep in mind that a search engine identifies any site in which the keyword or keywords that you have typed appear. (These sites are called *hits.*) Thus, a general keyword such as *Baltimore* could result in over a million hits. Because examining all these sites would be impossible, you need to focus your search, just as you would with your library's online catalog. By carrying out a **Boolean search,** combining keywords with AND, OR, or NOT (typed in capital letters), you can eliminate irrelevant hits from your search. For example, to find Web pages that have to do with Baltimore's economy, type *Baltimore AND economy.* Some search engines allow you to search using three or four keywords—*Baltimore AND history NOT agriculture,* for example. Focusing your searches in this way will enable you to retrieve information quickly and easily.

(3) Using Subject Guides

Some search engines, such as Yahoo!, About.com, and Look Smart, contain a **subject guide**—a list of general categories (*The Humanities, The Arts, Entertainment, Business,* and so on) from which you can choose. Each of these categories will lead you to more specific lists of categories and subcategories, until eventually you get to the topic you want. For example, clicking on *The Humanities* would lead you to *History,* which in turn would lead you to *American History* and eventually to *Vietnam War.* Although this is a time-consuming strategy for finding specific information, it can be an excellent tool for finding or narrowing a topic.

✔ **CHECKLIST: TIPS FOR EFFECTIVE WEB SEARCHES**

✔ **Choose the Right Search Engine** No one all-purpose search engine exists. Use a subject guide, such as the one available on Yahoo!, for exploratory research, and use a search engine, such as AltaVista, for more focused research.

continued on the following page

continued from the previous page

✔ **Choose Your Keywords Carefully** A search engine is only as good as the keywords you use. Choose keywords carefully.

✔ **Narrow Your Search** Carry out a Boolean search to make your searches more productive.

✔ **Check Your Spelling** If your search does not yield the results you expect, check to make sure you have spelled your search terms correctly. Even a one-letter mistake can confuse a search engine and cause it to retrieve the wrong information—or no information at all.

✔ **Include Enough Terms** If you are looking for information on housing, for example, search for several different variations of your keyword: *housing, houses, home buyer, buying houses, residential real estate,* and so on.

✔ **Consult the Help Screen** Most search engines have a help screen. If you have trouble with your search, do not hesitate to consult it. A little time spent here can save you a lot of time later.

✔ **Use More Than One Subject Guide or Search Engine** Different subject guides and search engines index different sites.

✔ **Add Useful Sites to Your Bookmark or Favorites List** Whenever you find a particularly useful Web site, **bookmark** it by selecting this option on the menu bar of your browser (with some browsers, such as *Microsoft Explorer,* this option is called *Favorites*). When you add a site to your bookmark list, you can return to the site whenever you want to by opening the bookmark menu and selecting it.

29b Using Other Internet Tools

In addition to the World Wide Web, the Internet contains a number of other components that you can use to gather and share information for your research.

(1) Using E-Mail

E-mail can be very useful to you as you do research. You can exchange ideas with classmates, ask questions of your instructors, and even conduct long-distance interviews. You can follow e-mail links in Web documents, and you can also transfer word-processing documents or other files (as e-mail attachments) from one computer to another.

(2) Using Listservs

Listservs (sometimes called **discussion lists**), electronic mailing lists to which you must subscribe, enable you to communicate with groups of people interested in particular topics (Vietnam veterans or sunken U-boats, for example). Individuals in a listserv send e-mails to a main e-mail address, and these messages are routed to all members in the group. Many listserv subscribers are experts who will often answer legitimate queries. Keep in mind, however, that anyone can join a listserv, so make sure you **evaluate** the information you get before you use it in your research.

See 29c

(3) Using Newsgroups

Like listservs, **newsgroups** are discussion groups. Unlike listserv messages, which are sent to you as e-mail, newsgroup messages are collected on the **Usenet** system, a global collection of news servers, where anyone can access them. In a sense, newsgroups function as gigantic bulletin boards where users post messages that others can read and respond to. Thus, newsgroups can be a source of specific information as well as suggestions about where to look for further information. Just as you would with a listserv, evaluate information you get from a newsgroup before you use it.

(4) Using Gopher, FTP, and Telnet

At one time, you needed special software to access gopher, telnet, and FTP. Now they can be accessed with most programs that access the Web.

Gopher is a tool that organizes textual information into hierarchical menus. You follow one menu to another until you get the information you want. Gopher gives you access to information about business, medicine, and engineering as well as access to archived newsgroups and electronic books and magazines.

FTP (file transfer protocol) enables you to transfer documents at high speed from one computer on the Internet to another. With FTP, you can get full text of books and articles as well as pictures. The most common use for FTP is for downloading updates from computer software manufacturers.

Telnet is a program that enables you to make a connection via telephone to another computer on the Internet. With telnet you can download anything from another host computer.

(5) Using MUDS, MOOS, IRCS, and Instant Messaging (Synchronous Communication)

With e-mails and listservs, there is a delay between the time a message is sent and the time it is received. **MUDS, MOOS, IRCS,** and **Instant Messaging** enable you to send and receive messages in real time. Communication is **synchronous;** that is, messages are sent and received as they are typed. Synchronous communication programs are being used more and more in college settings—for class discussions, online workshops, and collaborative projects.

29c Evaluating Internet Sites

Using the Web for your research has many advantages: it is easy, it is convenient, and it can yield a great deal of information, some of which you can get nowhere else. Even with these advantages, using the Web as a research tool can have some significant limitations.

**LIMITATIONS OF USING
THE WEB FOR RESEARCH**

- A Web search can yield more information than you can reasonably handle or properly evaluate.
- Because it is so convenient, Web research can cause you to ignore the resources in your college library. Many important and useful publications are available only in print and in library databases, not on the Web.
- A Web document may be unstable. Unlike print sources, Web documents can be altered at any time. For this reason, you cannot be sure that the information you see on a Web site will be there when you try to access it at a later date. (It is recommended that you keep copies of all Web documents that you use in your research.)
- Anyone can publish on the Web, so Web sites can vary greatly in reliability.
- Authorship and affiliation can sometimes be difficult or impossible to determine.

Because of these limitations, critical evaluation of Web site material is even more important than evaluation of more traditional print sources of information, such as books and journal articles. For this reason, you should carefully evaluate the content of any Web site for *accuracy, credibility, objectivity, currency, coverage* or *scope,* and *stability.*

Accuracy   Accuracy refers to the reliability of the material itself and to the use of proper documentation. Keep in mind that factual error—especially errors in facts that are central to the main point of the source—should cause you to question the reliability of the material you are reading.

- Is the text free of basic grammatical and mechanical errors?
- Does the site contain factual errors?
- Does the site provide a list of references?

- Are links available to other references?
- Can information be verified with print or other resources?

Credibility   *Credibility* refers to the credentials of the person or organization responsible for the site. Web sites operated by well-known institutions (the Smithsonian or the U.S. Department of Health and Human Services, for example) have built-in credibility. Those operated by individuals (private Web pages, for example) are often less reliable.

- Does the site list an author?
- Is the author a recognized authority in his or her field?
- Is the site **refereed?** That is, does an editorial board or a group of experts determine what material appears on the Web site?
- Does the organization sponsoring the Web site exist apart from its Web presence?
- Can you determine how long the Web site has existed?

☑ **CHECKLIST: DETERMINING THE LEGITIMACY OF AN ANONYMOUS OR QUESTIONABLE WEB SOURCE**

When a Web source is anonymous (or has an author whose name is not familiar to you), you have to take special measures to determine its legitimacy.

✔ ***Post a query.*** If you subscribe to a newsgroup or listserv, ask others in the group what they know about the source and its author.

✔ ***Follow the links.*** Follow the hypertext links in a document to other documents. If the links take you to legitimate sources, you know that the author is aware of these sources of information.

✔ ***Do a keyword search.*** Do a search using the name of the sponsoring organization or the article as key-words. Other documents (or citations in other works) may identify the author.

✔ ***Look at the URL.*** The last part of a Web site's URL can tell you whether the site is sponsored by a com-mercial entity (*.com*), a nonprofit organization (*.org*), an educational institution (*.edu*), the military (*.mil*), or a government agency (*.gov*). Knowing this infor-mation can tell you whether an organization is trying to sell you something (*.com*) or just providing infor-mation (*.edu* or *.org*).

Objectivity or Reasonableness   *Objectivity* or *reasonableness* refers to the degree of bias that a Web site exhibits. Some Web sites make no secret of their biases. They openly advocate a particular point of view or action, or they are clearly trying to sell something. Other Web sites may hide their biases. For example, a Web site may present itself as a source of factual information when it is actually advocating a political point of view.

- Does advertising appear in the text?
- Does a business, a political organization, or a special interest group sponsor the site?
- Are links provided to sites with a political agenda?
- Does the site express a particular viewpoint?
- Does the site contain links to other sites that express a particular viewpoint?

Currency *Currency* refers to how up-to-date the Web site is. The easiest way to assess a site's currency is to determine when it was last updated. Keep in mind, however, that even if the date on the site is current, the information that the site contains may not be.

- Does the site clearly identify the date it was created?
- Is the most recent update displayed?
- Are all the links to other sites still functioning?
- Is the actual information on the page up-to-date?

Coverage or Scope *Coverage* or *scope* refers to the comprehensiveness of the information on a Web site. More is not necessarily better, but some sites may be scanty or incomplete. Others may provide information that is no more than common knowledge. Still others may present discussions that may not be suitable for college-level research.

- Does the site provide in-depth coverage?
- Does the site provide information that is not available elsewhere?
- Does the site identify a target audience? Does this target audience suggest the site is appropriate for your research needs?

Stability *Stability* refers to whether or not the site is being maintained. A stable site will be around when you want to access it again. Web sites that are here today and gone tomorrow make it difficult for readers to check your sources or for you to obtain updated information.

- Has the site been active for a long period of time?
- Is the site updated regularly?
- Is the site maintained by a well-known, reliable organization—that is, one that is likely to be committed to financing the site?

29d Useful Web Sites

General Web Sites

- History Channel
  www.historychannel.com
- History Net
  www.TheHistoryNet.com
- History House
  www.historyhouse.com
- MSN Encarta
  Encarta.msn.com/encnet/refpages/artcenter.aspx?type=
  article&aoi=History
- Getty Images—Archive Films and Photos
  creative.gettyimages.com/archivefilms/?country=usa
- MSN Encarta—History and Historiography
  Encarta.msn.com/find/concise.asp?ti=761555707
- Academic Info—History Gateway
  www.academicinfo.net/hist.html
- History Text Archive
  historicaltextarchive.com
- History Today
  www.historytoday.com
- Horus's Web Links to History Resources
  www.ucr.edu/h-gig
- History Beat
  history.searchbeat.com
- Bit's O'History
  schoolmarm.org/historybits
- Library of Congress—Today in History
  lcweb2.loc.gov/ammem/today/today.html
- EyeWitness
  www.ibiscom.com
- Encyberpedia—History
  www.encyberpedia.com/history.htm
- Amazing Magnificent Cruise Through Time and History
  library.thinkquest.org/2834
- Spartacus Encyclopedias
  www.spartacus.schoolnet.co.uk/FWWtitle.html
- Today in History
  www.graphicjunction.communitech.net/today
- History Channel Traveler
  www.historytravel.com
- Real History Archives
  www.webcom.com/~lplease
- Random Walk Through the Twentieth Century
  ic.www.media.mit.edu/JBW
- HistoryNet—Today in History
  www.thehistorynet.com/today/today.htm
- National Museum of Natural History
  www.mnh.si.edu

- WWW-VL History Central Catalog
  www.ukans.edu/history/VL
- The Traveler
  hyperion.advanced.org/2840
- Smithsonian Institution
  www.si.edu

World History Websites

- World History Archives
  www.hartford-hwp.com/archives
- World History Association
  www.woodrow.org./teachers/world-history
- World History Compass
  www.worldhistorycompass.com
- History Wizard—Multimedia World History
  www.historywiz.com
- Ancient World Web
  www.julen.net/ancient
- Exploring Ancient World Cultures
  eawc.evansville.edu
- World History Links—Historyoftheworld.com
  www.historyoftheworld.com
- Bible World History Timeline
  agards.com/bible-study
- History of Africa—World History Archives
  www.hartford-hwp.com/archives/30/index.html
- The History Page
  www.scholiast.org/history

American History Websites

- History Place
  www.historyplace.com
- History Quiz
  www.geocities.com/Athens/Olympus/1834
- Increase and Diffusion
  www.si.edu/i+d
- Douglass
  douglass.speech.nwu.edu
- National Trust for Historic Preservation
  www.nationaltrust.org
- United States History
  www.academicinfo.net/histus.html
- Smithsonian National Museum of American History
  americanhistory.si.edu
- Early America—The Town Crier
  www.earlyamerica.com/towncrier
- U.S. History
  www.ushistory.org
- Historical Text Archive—Early U.S. Republic
  www.msstate.edu/Archives/History/USA/early_republic.early.html

Specific Websites

- Israel Government Gateway
  www.info.gov.il/eng/mainpage.asp
- Internet African History Sourcebook
  www.fordham.edu/halsall/africa/africasbook.html
- Russian-History.com
  www.russian-history.com
- Denver—Denver Museum of Nature and Science
  www.dmns.org
- Natural History Museum of Los Angeles County
  www.nhm.org
- Worldwide Museum of Natural History
  www.wmnh.com
- International Committee for the History of Technology
  www.icohtec.org
- NASA's History
  www.hq.nasa.gov/office/pao/History
- American Astronomical Society—History
  www.aas.org/~had/toc.html
- History of Mathematics—MacTutor Archive
  www-history.mcs.st-and.ac.uk/~history
- Fiber Optic History
  www.sff.net/people/Jeff.Hecht/history.html
- EH.Net—Economic History Services
  www.eh.net
- Hiroshima Prefecture
  www.city.hiroshima.jp
- American Museum of Natural History
  www.amnh.org
- Niels Bohr Institute
  www.nbi.dk
- BlackHistory.com
  www.blackhistory.com
- Cleveland Museum of Natural History
  www.cmnh.org
- American History X-Official
  www.historyx.com
- US Army—Center of Military History
  www.army.mil/cmh-pg/default.htm
- The Natural History Museum
  www.nhm.ac.uk
- National Women's History Project
  www.nwhp.org
- SHOT—Society for The History of Technology
  www.press.jhu.edu/associations/shot
- MacTutor History of Mathematics Archive
  www-history.mcs.st-andrews.ac.uk/history
- History of Korea
  kbsnt.kbs.co.kr/pr/history/contents.htm

- University of Mississippi—Historical Text Archive: Periodicals
  www.msstate.edu/Archives/History/Latin_America/Mexico/journal.html
- History Departments Around the World
  chnm.gmu.edu/history/depts./departments.qry?function=form
- To Fly is Everything
  Hawaii.cogsci.uiuc.edu/invent/airplanes.html
- University of Mississippi—Historical Text Archive: Mexico
  www.msstate.edu/Archives/History/Latin_America/Mexico/mexico.html
- Declaration of Causes of Seceding States
  funnelweb.utcc.utk.edu/~hoemann/reasons.html
- American Indian History Resources
  www.lang.osaka-u.ac.jp/~krkvls/history.html
- U.S. Army Center of Military History—Medal of Honor Citations
  imabbs.army.mil/cmh-pg/mohl.html
- Footlight Notes
  www.geocities.com/Broadway/Stage/4196
- Early Days of Persia/Iran—Some Historical Data
  www.cwi.nl/~keesh/Iran/beginning.html
- Iran Facts—Rulers and Dynasties
  www.cwi.nl/~keesh/Iran/dynasties.html
- MLB.com—World Series History
  mlb.mlb.com/NASApp/mlb/mlb/history/postseason/mlb_ws.jsp
- The U-boat War 1939–1945
  www.uboat.net
- History of Broadcasting
  www.people.memphis.edu/~mbensman/history1.html
- Salam Iran—History
  www.SalamIran.org/IranInfo/General/History
- Natural History Museums and Collections
  www.lib.washington.edu/sla/natmus.html
- Chandelle—A Journal of Aviation History
  www.concentric.net/~Rojo1
- Mexican Heads of State
  historicaltextarchive.com/sections.php?op=viewarticle&artid=154
- Representations of Astronomy
  cccw.adh.bton.ac.uk/schoolofdesign/MA.COURSE/LlnfDes21.html
- Korean History
  Socrates.Berkeley.edu/~korea/history.html
- The Prehistoric Archaeology of the Aegean
  devlab.cs.Dartmouth.edu/history/bronze_age
- Historical Documents—Thomas Legislative Information
  lcweb2.loc.gov/const/mdbquery.html
- History of Theatre
  www.ebicom.net/~tct/oftheatre.htm
- Infoplease—Black History Month
  looksmart.infoplease.com/spot/bhm1.html
- National Underground Railroad Freedom Center
  www.undergroundrailroad.org
- NYISE—African American History
  www.nyise.org/blackhistory

- CIA World Factbook—Gaza Strip
  www.odci.gov/cia/publications/factbook/geos/gz.html
- Ohio—Historical Society
  www.ohiokids.org/ohc
- First Thanksgiving—Plimoth Plantation
  www.plimoth.org/Library/Thanksgiving/firstT.htm
- History of India
  www.historyofindia.com
- MSN Encarta—Kosovo
  encarta.msn.com/find/concise.asp?ti=761579795
- Chinese Historical and Cultural Project
  www.chcp.org
- Laser History
  www.achilles.net/~jtalbot/history
- RMS Titanic, Inc.
  www.titanic-online.com
- CNN's Cold War Special
  www.cnn.com/SPECIALS/cold.war
- University of Wisconsin—The History of Cartography
  feature.geography.wisc.edu/histcart
- CivilWar.com
  www.civilwar.com
- Irish History
  www.vms.utexas.edu/jdana/irehist.html
- Smithsonian Institution—A Centennial Salute to Cinema
  photo2.si.edu/cinema/cinema.html
- Chronology of Russian History
  www.departments.bucknell.edu/russian/chrono.html
- Univ. of Michigan—Mother of All Art History Links Pages
  www.umich.edu/~hartspo/histart/mother
- Texas Historical Commission
  www.thc.state.tx.us
- Forum Romanum
  www.geocities.com/Athens/Forum/6946/rome.html
- On This Date In North American Indian History
  www.americanindian.net
- American Oriental Society
  www.umich.edu/~aos
- Brief History of the Internet
  www.isoc.org/internet-history/brief.html
- The Museum of Unnatural Mystery
  unmuseum.mus.pa.us
- National Women's Hall of Fame
  www.greatwomen.org
- National Numismatic Collection
  americanhistory.si.edu/csr/cadnnc.htm
- University of Pennsylvania—African Studies Center
  www.sas.upenn.edu/African_Studies/AS.html
- Calculating Machines
  www.webcom.com/calc

- Israel Ministry of Foreign Affairs
  www.israel.org
- Charles Babbage Institute
  www.cbi.umn.edu
- History of Money from Ancient Times to the Present Day
  www.ex.ac.uk/~Rdavies/arian/llyfr.html
- African History Timelines
  www.cocc.edu/cagatucci/classes/hum211/timelines/htimelinetoc.htm
- Smithsonian Computer History
  americanhistory.si.edu/csr/comphist
- Columbia University—Library: African Studies Internet Resources
  www.columbia.edu/cu/web/indiv/africa/curvl
- US Historical Documents Archive—Iroquois Constitution
  w3.one.net/~mweiler/ushda/iroconst.htm
- Ancestry.com
  www.ancestry.com
- U.S. Department of State—Gateway to African-American History
  usinfo.state.gov/usa/blackhis
- On This Day in Canadian History
  www1.simpatico.ca/cgi-bin/on_this_day
- Sisseton Wahpon Sioux Tribe
  www.swcc.cc.sd.us/swst.html
- Time Traveller
  ai.co.za/timetraveller
- The Sphinx Group—Egypt, Pyramids, Ancient History
  www.m-m.org/~jz/sphinx.html
- The World of Benjamin Franklin
  sln.fi.edu/franklin
- IEEE History Center
  www.ieee.org/history_center
- Olmecs
  udgftp.cencar.udg.mx/ingles/Precolombina/Olmecas/docs/olmin.html
- Prairie Band Potawatomi Home page
  www.public.iastate.edu/~jsmckinn/prairie_pot.html
- Egypt WWW Index
  pharos.bu.edu/Egypt/Home.html
- NASA Scientific and Technical Information Server
  www.sti.nasa.gov/STI-homepage.html
- Egyptian Pyramids Home Page
  www.tiac.net/users/ccstar/egypt
- NCN
  www.marekinc.com/NCN/html
- The Flags of the Native Peoples of the United States
  members.aol.com/Donh523/navapage
- Powering a Generation of Change
  www.si.edu/organiza/museums/nmah/csr/powering
- Welcome to Cameroon
  www.rt66.com/~telp/cam.htm
- The History of the Cherokee
  www.phoenix.net/~martikw

Using Internet Sources

- Islamweb
  islamweb.net/pls/iweb/misc1.ehome
- History of World Series
  www.sportingnews.com/archives/worldseries/side.html
- History and Customs of Halloween
  wilstar.com/holidays/hallown.htm
- Africa South of the Sahara
  www-sul.Stanford.edu/depts./ssrg/Africa/guide2.html
- Ground Zero
  groundzero.nyc.ny.us
- Islam Online
  www.islam-online.net
- The Knesset—The Parliament of Israel
  www.knesset.gov.il

Educators/Teachers Web sites
- Women in World History Curriculum
  www.womeninworldhistory.com
- People's Century—PBS
  www.pbs.org/wgbh/peoplescentury
- NM's Creative Impulse
  history.Evansville.net
- National Center for History in the Schools
  www.sscnet.ucla.edu/nchs/
- History Departments Around the World
  chnm.gmu.edu/history/depts
- HistorySeek!
  www.historyseek.com
- Increase and Diffusion
  www.si.edu/i+d
- Eighteenth-Century Studies
  www.hss.cmu.edu/18th
- NARA Archival Information Locator
  www.archives.gov/research_room/arc/index.html
- Concord Review
  www.tcr.org
- UCMP—Artifact and Historical Collection Catalogs
  www.ucmp.berkeley.edu/collections/otherart.html
- Academic Info—European History
  www.academicinfo.net/histeuro.html
- History Television
  www.historytelevision.com
- American and British History Resources
  www.libraries.rutgers.edu/rul/rr_gateway/research_guides/history/references
- American Memory
  memory.loc.gov
- History and Theory
  www.historyandtheory.org
- K–12 History on the Internet Resource Guide
  www.xs4all.nl/~swanson/history

- Internet Modern History Sourcebook
  www.fordham.edu/halsall/mod/modsbook.html
- Academic Info—Ancient History Resources
  www.academicinfo.net/histanc.html
- History Net–National History Day
  www.thehistorynet.com/NationalHistoryDay
- National Council for History Education
  www.history.org.nche
- GAES—American History for Students
  www.geocities.com/Athens/Academy/6617/amlist.html
- Global History Consortium—Teaching World History
  www.stockton.edu/~gilmorew/consort/index.html
- Mister History's Home Page
  homepage.usr.com/m/mrhistory
- Washington State Historical Society
  www.wshs.org
- Academic Info—African Studies
  www.academicinfo.net/histafrica.html
- Daily Life in Ancient Civilizations
  members.aol.com/Donnclass/indexlife.html
- History—Schoolwork.org
  www.schoolwork.org/history.html

CHAPTER 30

INTEGRATING SOURCES AND AVOIDING PLAGIARISM

30a Integrating Source Material into Your Writing

Weave paraphrases, summaries, and quotations of source material smoothly into your paper, adding your own analysis or explanation to increase coherence and to show the relevance of your sources to the points you are making.

(1) Integrating Quotations

Quotations should never be awkwardly dropped into your paper, leaving the exact relationship between the quotation and your point unclear. Instead, use a brief introductory remark to provide a context for the quotation.

CORRECT: "Hooker sent his two brigades over the ground already covered with the fallen, and added to the heaps of dead" (Harry Hansen, *The Civil War: A History* [NY: Penguin, 1991], 287).

UNACCEPTABLE: Confederate ground forces were dominant during the Battle of Fredricksburg. "Hooker sent his two brigades over the ground already covered with the fallen, and added to the heaps of dead."[1]

ACCEPTABLE: Confederate ground forces, dominant during the Battle of Fredericksburg, "added to the heaps of dead."[1]

Whenever possible, use an **identifying tag** (a phrase that identifies the source) to introduce the quotation.

IDENTIFYING TAG: According to Hansen , the Confederate ground forces, dominant during the Battle of Fredericksburg, "added to the heaps of dead."[1]

INTEGRATING SOURCE MATERIAL INTO YOUR WRITING

To make sure all your sentences do not sound the same, experiment with different methods of integrating source material into your paper.

- Vary the verbs you use to introduce a source's words or ideas (instead of repeating *says*).

acknowledges	discloses	implies
suggests	observes	notes
concludes	believes	comments
insists	explains	claims
predicts	summarizes	illustrates
reports	finds	proposes
warns	concurs	speculates
admits	affirms	indicates

- Vary the placement of the identifying tag, putting it sometimes in the middle or at the end of the quoted material instead of always at the beginning.

QUOTATION WITH IDENTIFYING TAG IN MIDDLE:
"The Confederates," writes Hansen, "had mastery over the field."[1]

PARAPHRASE WITH IDENTIFYING TAG AT END:
Confederate ground forces dominated the Federals during the Battle of Fredericksburg, according to Hansen.[1]

PUNCTUATING IDENTIFYING TAGS

Whether or not you use a comma with an identifying tag depends on where you place it in the sentence. If the identifying tag immediately precedes a quotation, use a comma.

continued on the following page

continued from the previous page

> As Hansen points out, "The Confederates had mastery over the field."[1]

If the identifying tag does not immediately precede a quotation, do not use a comma.

> Hansen points out that Confederate soldiers "had mastery over the field."[1]

Substitutions or Additions within Quotations When you make changes or additions to make a quotation fit into your paper, acknowledge your changes by enclosing them in brackets.

ORIGINAL QUOTATION: "Their arena was the marketplace, in which they detected a unique egalitarianism transcending cultural and political differences." (Alan M. Kraut, "Consensus and Pluralism: The Popular Will and the American People 1820–1940," in *The Will of the People: The Legacy of George Mason,* ed. George R. Johnson, Jr. [Fairfax, VA: George Mason University Press, 1991], 76.)

QUOTATION REVISED TO SUPPLY AN ANTECEDENT FOR A PRONOUN: "Their [advertisers'] arena was the marketplace, in which they detected a unique egalitarianism transcending cultural and political differences."[1]

QUOTATION REVISED TO CHANGE A CAPITAL TO A LOWERCASE LETTER: Advertisers understood how to find buyers for their goods because "[t]heir arena was the marketplace, in which they detected a unique egalitarianism transcending cultural and political differences."[1]

Omissions within Quotations When you delete unnecessary or irrelevant words, substitute an **ellipsis** (three spaced periods) for the deleted words.

See 20f

ORIGINAL: "In the generation after 1903, the year the Wright brothers attached a motor to a glider, a succession of advances in the technology of flight had enabled the United States to begin a global airline." (Donald W. White, *The American Century: The Rise and Decline of the United States as a World Power* [New Haven, CT: Yale University Press, 1996], 170.)

QUOTATION REVISED TO ELIMINATE UNNECESSARY WORDS: "In the generation after 1903, ... a succession of advances in the technology of flight had enabled the United States to begin a global airline."[1]

OMISSIONS WITHIN QUOTATIONS

Be sure that you do not misrepresent quoted material when you delete words from it. For example, do not say, "advances in . . . technology . . . had enabled the United States to begin a global airline" when the original quotation is "advances in *the* technology *of flight* had enabled the United States to begin a global airline."

For treatment of long quotations, see **19a.**

(2) Integrating Paraphrases and Summaries

Introduce paraphrases and summaries with identifying tags, and end them with appropriate documentation. Doing so allows readers to differentiate your ideas from the ideas of your sources.

MISLEADING (IDEAS OF SOURCE BLEND WITH IDEAS OF WRITER): Adams's essays demonstrated his discontent in terms that suggested to many unbridled emotion rather than concerned outspokenness. Some people felt he should be censored. But not everyone agreed. Some believed Adams's restraint suggested his *Patriot* essays were not a product of uncontrolled emotion. When the *Patriot* essays are compared with the 1801 draft of his response to Hamilton's pamphlet, the 1809 essays seem relatively tame.[1]

REVISED WITH IDENTIFYING TAG (IDEAS OF SOURCE DIFFERENTIATED FROM IDEAS OF WRITER): Adams's essays demonstrated his discontent in terms that suggested to many unbridled emotion rather than concerned outspokenness. Some people felt he should be censored. But not everyone agreed. <u>According to Freeman in *Affairs of Honor*</u> , some believed Adams's restraint suggested his *Patriot* essays were not a product of uncontrolled emotion. When the *Patriot* essays are compared with the 1801 draft of his response to Hamilton's pamphlet, the 1809 essays seem relatively tame.[1]

30b Avoiding Plagiarism

Plagiarism is presenting another person's words or ideas—either accidentally or intentionally—as though they are your own. In general, you must provide **documentation** for all direct quotations, as well as for every opinion, judgment, and insight of someone else that you summarize or paraphrase. You must also document tables, graphs, charts, and statistics taken from a source.

See Pt. 7

Of course, certain information need not be documented: **common knowledge** (information that is generally known), familiar sayings and well-known quotations, and the results of your own original research (interviews and surveys, for example). Information that is in dispute or that is one person's original contribution, however, must be acknowledged. For example, you need not document the fact that John F. Kennedy graduated from Harvard in 1949 or that he was elected president in 1960. You must, however, document a historian's evaluation of Kennedy's performance as president or a researcher's recent revelations about Kennedy's private life.

You can avoid plagiarism by using documentation wherever it is required and by following these guidelines.

(1) Enclose Borrowed Words in Quotation Marks

ORIGINAL: "Lincoln's policies were rooted in Hamilton and Clay's American System, and his Hamiltonianism was evident in his support of internal improvements such as railroad and canal expansion and land-grant colleges. Most important, his celebration of the wage laborer as against the slave in an increasingly industrial America was decidedly Hamiltonian. Yet Lincoln was relatively silent about Hamilton." (Stephen F. Knott, *Alexander Hamilton and the Persistence of Myth* [Lawrence: University Press of Kansas, 2002], 54.)

PLAGIARISM: Stephen F. Knott points out that many of Lincoln's policies were based on Hamilton's beliefs, yet Lincoln was relatively silent about Hamilton.[1]

Even though the student writer does include a superscript number referring readers to his bibliography, where he lists the source of his information, he uses the source's exact words without placing them in quotation marks.

CORRECT (BORROWED WORDS IN QUOTATION MARKS): Stephen F. Knott points out that although many of Lincoln's policies were based on Hamilton's beliefs, "<u>Lincoln was relatively silent about Hamilton.</u>"[1]

CORRECT (PARAPHRASE): Stephen F. Knott points out that many of Lincoln's policies were based on Hamilton's beliefs <u>but that Lincoln did not attribute those ideas to Hamilton</u>.[1]

(2) Do Not Imitate a Source's Syntax and Phrasing

ORIGINAL: "The Constitution created a lower house of the Congress chosen by direct popular vote, thereby preserving

the most traditional channel for the expression of the will of
the people in the affairs of government." (Thad Tate, "The Will
of the People in Eighteenth-Century America," in *The Will of
the People: The Legacy of George Mason,* ed. George R. Johnson,
Jr. [Fairfax, VA: George Mason University, 1991], 41.)

PLAGIARISM: As Thad Tate observes, the Constitution established a lower house of Congress selected by direct popular vote, thereby maintaining the traditional method of
expressing the will of the people in government affairs.[1]

Although this student does cite her source and does not use its
exact words, she closely imitates the original's syntax and phrasing, simply substituting synonyms for the author's words.

**CORRECT (PARAPHRASE IN WRITER'S OWN WORDS; ONE
DISTINCTIVE PHRASE PLACED IN QUOTATION MARKS):**
Thad Tate observes that the Constitution allows for one house
of Congress to be selected by a vote of the people, and he be-
lieves that this selection reflects the most time-honored way
of respecting "the will of the people."[1]

(3) Document Statistics Obtained
from a Source

Although many people assume that statistics are common
knowledge, statistics are usually the result of original research
and must therefore be documented.

CORRECT: According to recent estimates, over two hundred ships were destroyed on the eastern seaboard between
January and April of 1942.[1]

(4) Differentiate Your Words and Ideas
from Those of Your Source

ORIGINAL: "The magic of the land remained a theme of
modern American life, as it had since the early settlements.
Immense virgin spaces and a frontier to conquer were parts
of that theme." (Donald W. White, *The American Century*
[New Haven, CT: Yale University Press, 1996], 129.)

PLAGIARISM: In modern American life, the mystical appeal
of the land continued to be an important theme, as it always
had. This appeal was based on "immense virgin spaces and a
frontier to conquer."[1]

Because the student writer does not differentiate his ideas from
those of his source, it appears that only the quotation in the last
sentence is borrowed when, in fact, the first sentence also owes a
debt to the original. The student should have clearly identified
the boundaries of the borrowed material by introducing it with

an identifying tag and ending with documentation. (Note that a quotation always requires separate documentation.)

> **CORRECT:** According to Donald White, in modern American life, the mystical appeal of the land continued to be an important theme, as it always had. This appeal was based on "immense virgin spaces and a frontier to conquer."[1]

PLAGIARISM AND INTERNET SOURCES

Any time you download text from the Internet, you risk committing plagiarism. To avoid the possibility of plagiarism, follow these guidelines.

- Download information into individual files so that you can keep track of your sources.

- Do not simply cut and paste blocks of downloaded text into your paper; summarize or paraphrase this material first.

- If you do record the exact words of your source, enclose them in quotation marks.

- Whether your information is from e-mails, online discussion groups, listservs, or Web sites, give proper credit by providing appropriate documentation.

CHAPTER 31

GLOSSARY OF TERMS

Archive   Any place, including the World Wide Web, where public records or historical documents are preserved.

Atlas   A collection of maps, bound and often including illustrations and other informative visual aids.

Autobiography   A written record, made by the person himself or herself, of that person's life.

Bibliography   A list of works related to a particular subject, period, or author. For students, a list of works referred to or consulted in a research paper. Some bibliographies are annotated with descriptive or critical notes.

Biography   A record, written by someone else, of a person's life.

Bookmark   A mechanism on your browser for recording the URL of a particular site for future use.

Catalog   A listing of books or other items, arranged systematically and with descriptive details.

Chatroom   A place on the Web where you can enter into a conversation with others, often focusing on a particular topic.

Citation   A reference usually in the form of a footnote or endnote, or a source of information used in writing a paper.

Common knowledge   The information, data, or evidence general enough and well known enough to be possessed by most, if not all, people interested in a specific topic. Common knowledge does not need to be documented.

Database   A large accumulation of information on a particular subject or subjects organized for quick retrieval.

Directory   A list of files and folders that facilitate quick searches of subjects for research. A kind of search engine.

Documentation   The use of evidence to support a general statement.

Draft   A preliminary version of a paper.

Endnotes   The notes documenting information in the text and corresponding to reference numbers in the text that appear at the end of a research paper, at the end of a chapter, or at the end of an article in a journal. For book manuscripts, Chicago documentation style prefers use of endnotes rather than footnotes.

Footnotes   The notes documenting information in the text and corresponding to reference numbers in the text that appear at the bottom (foot) of a page.

Full text   The electronic databases that contain the complete text of sources rather than merely abstracts or information for finding sources.

Historiography   The study of changes over time in methods, interpretations, and conclusions reached by historians.

Home page   The first page of a Web site. Most often, a home page has links to other parts of the site and to other sites.

Hypertext link (often referred to as a link)   A connection between two different pages on the World Wide Web that appears on your screen as an icon or highlighted or underlined text to be clicked on.

Keyword   A word or phrase that reflects fundamental aspects of a topic to be researched; keywords enable online catalogs and electronic databases on the Web to be searched for relevant information.

Library catalog   An organizational system for library holdings (most are now electronic).

Listserv   An electronic form of communication (like e-mail) in which subscribers with a shared interest in a topic communicate. Often, past communications are preserved so that previous messages can be read.

Microfiche   The sheets of microfilm containing pages of information printed in reduced form.

Microfilm   A film with a reduced photographic record of print or other graphic matter.

Online catalog   An electronic listing of items held in a library or libraries accessible from a computer.

Paraphrase   A restatement giving information in different words.

Periodical   A newspaper, magazine, scholarly journal, or other publication that is published at fixed intervals.

Periodical database   The electronic source for a listing of a large collection of articles from journals, magazines, or newspapers.

Plagiarism   The illegal and unethical use of ideas and words of another as one's own. If an idea or words are not common knowledge, they must be documented.

Primary source   The firsthand evidence in the words of someone who either participated in or witnessed the events described or who received information from direct participants.

Quotation   The exact words of a source. Direct quotations must be documented properly.

Search engine   A computer application that enables users to locate relevant sites by use of keyword searches.

Secondary source   The findings of someone who has researched primary evidence on an event.

Subject headings   The terms used in catalogs to describe the contents of a library's or Web site's holdings. *Library of Congress Subject Headings* is an excellent source.

Table   A condensation of a relatively large amount of information into rows and columns for easy access; most often accompanied by a brief explanation in the text both before and after. Small amounts of information may be summarized in the text itself rather than in a table.

URL   The "Uniform Resource Locator" is an electronic address for a Web site.

Web browser   An application that enables users to view a variety of subjects on World Wide Web sites.

World Wide Web   The part of the Internet that connects texts, including images and sound, by means of embedded links.

PART 7

DOCUMENTING SOURCES

DIRECTORY OF CHICAGO STYLE ENDNOTE AND BIBLIOGRAPHY ENTRIES

Entries for Books

Entries for Articles

Entries for Other Sources

Entries for Electronic Sources

CHAPTER 32

CHICAGO DOCUMENTATION STYLE

32a Using Chicago Documentation Style

The Chicago Manual of Style (CMS) is used in history and some social science and humanities disciplines. **Chicago documentation style*** has two parts: notes at the end of the paper (endnotes) and a list of bibliographic citations. (Although Chicago documentation style encourages the use of endnotes, it also allows the use of footnotes at the bottom of the page.)

(1) Endnotes and Footnotes

The notes format calls for a **superscript** (raised numeral) in the text after source material you have either quoted or referred to. This numeral, which is placed after all punctuation marks except dashes, corresponds to the numeral that accompanies the note.

Endnote and Footnote Format: Chicago Style
In the Text
By November of 1942, the Allies had proof that the Nazis were engaged in the systemic killing of Jews.[1]
In the Note
1. David S. Wyman, *The Abandonment of the Jews: America and the Holocaust 1941–1945* (New York: Pantheon Books, 1984), 65.

(2) Bibliography

In addition to the heading *Bibliography,* Chicago style allows *Selected Bibliography, Works Cited, Literature Cited, References,* and *Sources Consulted.*

Sample Chicago Style Entries: Books   Capitalize the first, last, and all major words of titles and subtitles. Although underlining to indicate italics is acceptable, Chicago style recommends the use of italics for titles.

1. A Book by One Author
   Endnote
   1. Herbert J. Gans, *The Urban Villagers,* 2nd ed. (New York: Free Press, 1982), 100.

---

*Chicago style follows the guidelines set in *The Chicago Manual of Style*, 15th ed. (Chicago: University of Chicago Press, 2003).

Bibliography

Gans, Herbert J. *The Urban Villagers.* 2nd ed. New York: Free Press, 1982.

2. A Book by Two or Three Authors
Endnote

2. Robert W. Tucker and David C. Hendrickson, *Empire of Liberty: The Statecraft of Thomas Jefferson* (New York: Oxford University Press, 1990), 105.

Bibliography

Tucker, Robert W., and David C. Hendrickson. *Empire of Liberty: The Statecraft of Thomas Jefferson.* New York: Oxford University Press, 1990.

3. A Book by More Than Three Authors
Endnote

3. Robert E. Spiller et al., eds., *Literary History of the United States* (New York: Macmillan, 1974), 24.

Bibliography

Spiller, Robert E., et al., eds. *Literary History of the United States.* New York: Macmillan, 1974.

4. An Edited Book
Endnote

4. Marion Hill Fitzpatrick, *Letters to Amanda: The Civil War Letters of Marion Hill Fitzpatrick, Army of Northern Virginia,* ed. Jeffrey C. Lowe (Macon, GA: Mercer University Press, 1998), 98.

Bibliography

Fitzpatrick, Marion Hill. *Letters to Amanda: The Civil War Letters of Marion Hill Fitzpatrick, Army of Northern Virginia.* Edited by Jeffrey C. Lowe. Macon, GA: Mercer University Press, 1998.

5. A Translation
Endnote

5. Abdallah Frangi, *The PLO and Palestine,* trans. Paul Knight (London: Zed Books, 1983), 28.

Bibliography

Fangi, Abdallah. *The PLO and Palestine.* Translated by Paul Knight. London: Zed Books, 1983.

6. A Chapter in a Book or an Essay in an Anthology
Endnote

6. Peter Kidson, "Architecture and City Planning," in *The Legacy of Greece,* ed. M. I. Finley (New York: Oxford University Press, 1981), 379.

Bibliography

Kidson, Peter. "Architecture and City Planning." In *The Legacy of Greece,* ed. M. I. Finley, 376–400. New York: Oxford University Press, 1981.

7. A Multivolume Work
Endnote

7. Kenneth P. Williams, *Lincoln Finds a General: A Military Study of the Civil War* (New York: Macmillan, 1949), 1:221.

Bibliography

Williams, Kenneth P. *Lincoln Finds a General: A Military Study of the Civil War,* vol. 1. New York: Macmillan, 1949.

Sample Chicago Style Entries: Articles

8. An Encyclopedia or Dictionary Entry
Endnote

8. *Encyclopedia Britannica,* 15th ed., s.v. "War of 1812."

Bibliography

Well-known reference works are usually not cited in bibliographies.

9. An Article in a Scholarly Journal with Continuous Pagination through an Annual Volume
Endnote

9. E. Lawrence Abel, "And the Generals Sang," *Civil War Times* 39 (Fall 2000): 46.

Bibliography

Abel, E. Lawrence. "And the Generals Sang." *Civil War Times* 39 (Fall 2000): 45–57.

10. An Article in a Scholarly Journal with Separate Pagination in Each Issue
Endnote

10. Daniel Horodsky, "How U.S. Merchant Marines Fared During WWII," *Insight on the News* 16, no. 1 (2000): 51.

Bibliography

Horodsky, Daniel. "How U.S. Merchant Marines Fared During WWII." *Insight on the News* 16, no. 1 (2000): 46–55.

11. An Article in a Weekly Magazine
Endnote

11. Ira Silverman, "An American Terrorist," *New Yorker,* August 5, 2002, 26.

Bibliography

Silverman, Ira. "An American Terrorist." *New Yorker,* August 5, 2002, 26–31.

12. An Article in a Monthly Magazine
Endnote

12. Leander Stillwell, "In the Ranks at Shiloh," *Journal of the Illinois State Historical Society,* April 1923, 460.

Bibliography

Stillwell, Leander. "In the Ranks at Shiloh," *Journal of the Illinois State Historical Society,* April 1923, 460.

13. An Article in a Newspaper
Endnote

13. Raymond Bonner, "A Guatemalan General's Rise to Power," *New York Times,* July 21,1982, sec. 3A.

Bibliography

Bonner, Raymond. "A Guatemalan General's Rise to Power." *New York Times,* July 21, 1982, sec. 3A.

14. A Book Review
Endnote

14. Herman Viola, review of *The Yellowstone Story,* by Aubrey L. Haines, *New Yorker,* December 30, 1980, 169.

Bibliography

Viola, Herman. Review of *The Yellowstone Story,* by Aubrey L. Haines. *New Yorker,* December 30, 1980, 169.

Sample Chicago Style Entries: Other Sources

15. A Government Document
Endnote

15. U.S. Department of State, *Foreign Relations Volume 17, Arab-Israeli Dispute,* 1964–1967 (Washington, DC: GPO, 2000), 827.

Bibliography

U.S. Department of State. *Foreign Relations Volume 17, Arab-Israeli Dispute,* 1964–1967. Washington, DC: GPO, 2000.

16. A Pamphlet
Endnote

16. Margaret T. Crane, *Poverty in Eastern North Carolina* (Greenville, NC: East Carolina University, 1988).

Bibliography

Crane, Margaret T. *Poverty in Eastern North Carolina.* Greenville, NC: East Carolina University, 1988.

17. A Personal Interview
Endnote

17. Cornel West, interview by author, tape recording, June 8, 1994. St. Louis, MO.

Bibliography

West, Cornel. Interview by author. Tape recording. June 8, 1994, St. Louis, MO.

18. A Published Interview
Endnote

18. Herman J. Viola, interview by Stephen Goode, *Insight on the News,* January 3, 2000, 36.

Bibliography

Viola, Herman J. Interview by Stephen Goode. *Insight on the News,* January 3 ,2000, 36–40.

19. A Letter
Endnote

19. James T. Cheatham, letter to author, April 21, 2000.

Bibliography

Cheatham, James T. Letter to author. April 21, 2000.

20. An Unpublished Dissertation
Endnote
20. Mattie Russell, "William Holland Thomas, White Chief of the North Carolina Cherokees" (PhD diss., Duke University, 1956). 140–42.

Bibliography
Russell, Mattie. "William Hollan Thomas, White Chief of the North Carolina Cherokees." PhD diss., Duke University, 1956.

21. A Film or Videotape
Endnote
21. Louis J. Mihalyi, *Landscapes of Zambia, Central Africa,* Santa Barbara, CA: (Visual Education, 1975), slides, 25 min.

Bibliography
Louis J. Mihalyi. *Landscapes of Zambia, Central Africa.* Santa Barbara, CA: Visual Education, 1975. Slides. 25 min.

22. A Recording
Endnote
22. Bob Marley, "Crisis," *Bob Marley and the Wailers,* Kava Island Records compact disc, 423 095-3.

Bibliography
Marley, Bob. "Crisis." *Bob Marley and the Wailers.* Kava Island Records 423 095-3. Compact disc.

Sample Chicago Style Entries: Electronic Sources

The Chicago Manual of Style, 15th Edition, recommends styling electronic references (both notes and bibliographies) the same way as print references, with the URL added after the citation. For time-sensitive material, you may include the access date within parentheses after the URL.

23. A Web Site
Endnote
23. Chris Keller, Elizabeth Simpson, Chad Powell, *The Battle of Bull Run or Manassas,* September 16, 2002. http://www.pekin.net/pekin108/edison/projects/bullrun.html.

Bibliography
Keller, Chris, Elizabeth Simpson, Chad Powell. *The Battle of Bull Run or Manassas.* September 16, 2002. http://www.pekin.net/pekin108/edison/ projects/bullrun.html.

24. A Document from a Database
Endnote
24. Cheryl A. Wells, "Battle Time: Gender, Modernity, and Confederate Hospitals," *Journal of Social History* 35, no. 2 (2001): 409. *Expanded Academic ASAP,* InfoTrac.

Bibliography
Wells, Cheryl A. "Battle Time: Gender, Modernity, and Confederate Hospitals." *Journal of Social History* 35, no.2 (2001): 409. *Expanded Academic ASAP,* InfoTrac.

25. An E-mail Message

Endnote

25. Carl Swanson, "Sample Assignments for Writing in History," December 19, 2002, personal e-mail.

Bibliography

Swanson, Carl. "Sample Assignments for Writing in History." December 19, 2002. Personal e-mail.

26. A Listserv Message

Endnote

26. Tim Runyan, runyant@mail.ecu.edu "The Merrimac," January 27, 2003, majordemo@ns.planet.gen.nz.

Bibliography

Runyan, Tim.runyant@mail.ecu.edu, "The Merrimac." January 27, 2003. majordemo@ns.planet.gen.nz.

27. An E-book

Endnote

27. J. Wesley Bond, "Minnesota and Its Resources" in *Making of America,* 2002, http: www.hti.umich.edu/cgi/t/text/text-idx.

Bibliography

Bond, J. Wesley. "Minnesota and Its Resources" in *Making of America,* 2002, 115–37. http:www.hti.umich.edu/cgi/t/text/ text-idx.

28. A Gopher Site

Endnote

28. "Democratic Party Platform, 1860," June 18, 1860, wiretap.spies.com.

Bibliography

"Democratic Party Platform, 1860." June 18, 1860. wiretap.spies.com.

29. An Article in an Online Scholarly Journal

Endnote

29. B. Fay, "Unconventional History." *History and Theory* 41, no. 2 (2002): 175. http://www.ingenta.com/isis/general/lsp/ingenta.

Bibliography

Fay, B. "Unconventional History." *History and Theory* 41, no. 2 (2002): 175. http://www.ingenta.com/isis/general/lsp/ingenta.

Sample Chicago Style Entries: Electronic Sources

30. Computer Software

Endnote

30. Reunion: The Family Tree Software vers. 2.0 for Macintosh (Cambridge, MA: Lester Productions).

Bibliography

Reunion: The Family Tree Software. Vers. 2.0 for Macintosh. Cambridge, MA: Lester Productions.

32b Chicago Style Manuscript Guidelines

✔ CHECKLIST: TYPING YOUR PAPER

- ✔ On the title page include the full title of your paper as well as your name. You may also be asked to include the course title, the instructor's name, and the date.

- ✔ Type your paper with a one-inch margin at the top, at the bottom, and on both sides.

- ✔ Double-space your paper throughout.

- ✔ Indent the first line of each paragraph five spaces. Set off a long prose quotation (eight or more typed lines or more than one paragraph) from the text by indenting ½ inch (about ten spaces) from the left-hand margin. If the quotation is a full paragraph, include the paragraph indentation.

- ✔ Number all pages consecutively in the upper right-hand corner, one-half inch from the top, flush right. Although it is not required, you may include your name before the page number. Although the title page is counted as page 1, it is not numbered. The first full page of the paper will be numbered page 2.

- ✔ Use superscript numbers to indicate in-text citations. Type superscript numbers at the end of cited material (quotations, paraphrases, or summaries). Leave no space between the superscript number and the preceding letter or punctuation mark.

- ✔ if you use source material in your paper, use **Chicago documentation style**.

See 33a

✔ CHECKLIST: PREPARING CHICAGO STYLE ENDNOTES

- ✔ Begin the endnotes on a new page after the last page of the paper.
- ✔ Center the title *Notes* one inch from the top of the page.

continued on the following page

continued from the previous page

✔ Number the page on which the endnotes appear as the next page of the paper.

✔ Type and number notes in the order in which they appear in the paper, beginning with number 1.

✔ Type the note number on (not above) the line, followed by a period and one space.

✔ Indent the first line of each note ¼ inch (about four spaces); type subsequent lines flush with the left-hand margin.

✔ Double-space within and between entries.

SUBSEQUENT REFERENCES TO THE SAME WORK

In the first reference to a work, use the full citation; in subsequent references to the same work, list the author's last name, followed by a comma and an abbreviated title and then by a comma and a page number.

First Note on Espinoza

1. J. M. Espinoza, *The First Expedition of Vargas in New Mexico, 1692* (Albuquerque: University of New Mexico Press, 1949), 10–12.

Subsequent Note

5. Epinoza, *First Expedition,* 29.

NOTE: *The Chicago Manual of Style* allows the use of the abbreviation *ibid.* ("in the same place") for subsequent references to the same work as long as there are no intervening references. *Ibid.* takes the place of the author's name and the work's title—but not the page number.

First Note on Espinoza

1. J. M. Espinoza, *The First Expedition of Vargas in New Mexico, 1692* (Albuquerque: University of New Mexico Press, 1949), 10–12.

Subsequent Note on Espinoza

2. Espinoza, *First Expedition,* 23.

Note Immediately Following an Espinoza Note

3. Ibid., 27

✓ CHECKLIST: PREPARING THE CHICAGO STYLE BIBLIOGRAPHY

✔ Type entries on a separate page after the endnotes.
✔ List entries alphabetically according to the author's last name.
✔ Type the first line of each entry flush with the left-hand margin; indent subsequent lines ¼ inch (about four spaces).
✔ Double-space the bibliography within and between entries.

32c Sample Chicago Style Research Paper

The following is a paper that uses Chicago Style documentation and includes a title page, endnotes, and a bibliography.

Forgotten Heroes: The Buffalo Soldiers

By

Angela M. Womack

Title centered and capitalized, followed by name

American History 301

Dr. Adkins

December 3, 2003

Course title
Instructor
Date

Indent →
5 spaces

In September or 1879, the U.S. Ninth Cavalry was tracking the Apache chief Victorio through the harsh New Mexico terrain. According to Frank Schubert, the Ninth had been stationed all over the western frontier and had tracked Victorio and his raiding parties for some time, but they now felt that they might finally be catching up to him. Unfortunately, they were correct. On September 18, 150 Apaches ambushed elements of the Ninth and pinned them down in a canyon at the head of Las Animas Creek. Surrounded, outnumbered, and pinned down by the Apaches, the men of the Ninth held the Apaches at bay and waited for the rest of the regiment. One of those soldiers was John Denny. During the firefight, Denny dropped his rifle and ran to a soldier named Freeland, who had been wounded and lying in the open. Denny picked Freeland up and carried him back under cover. Freeland lived, and Denny was miraculously uninjured. For his courage under fire, Denny would receive the Medal of Honor.[1]

Superscript
numbers

John Denny was hardly alone in displaying courage and valor. The Ninth Cavalry, one of four regiments made up of African American volunteers, was formed after the Civil War and nicknamed "Buffalo Soldiers" by the Indians.[2] Over the course of thirty years, twenty-three Buffalo Soldiers earned the Medal of Honor while serving all over the frontier and in the Spanish-American War.[3] According to his-

3

torian William Katz, from the end of the Civil War until the end of the nineteenth century, they constituted twenty percent of all U.S. forces in outposts scattered over Kansas, Texas, Utah, New Mexico, Arizona, Wyoming, and North and South Dakota.[4] As Katz notes, these men faced the hardships of the West, fought in countless engagements with hostile Indians and outlaws, built the forts that served as outposts of safety and civilization, and helped map the trails and lay the railroads and telegraph wires. The soldiers of the Twenty-fourth and Twenty-fifth Infantry regiments and Ninth and Tenth Cavalry regiments did all this despite the cloud of racism and bigotry that followed them wherever they went. In spite of this harsh treatment, the Buffalo Soldiers served their country and acted as pioneers not only in the American West but also in the struggle for racial equality.

    Thesis statement

As Michael T. Lubbrage explains, with the end of the Civil War, "Go West, young man" became America's unofficial motto. Since the original thirteen colonies had been established, Lubbrage notes, Americans had expanded steadily toward the Pacific Ocean. After the war, the government began encouraging westward settlement by promising cheap land and helping to expand transportation and communication across the country. According to Lubbrage, this westward expansion was driven by a

4

Figure 1 The Ninth Cavalry posing for a photo in Pine Ridge, South Dakota, during the winter of 1890. © The Granger Collection.

belief in Manifest Destiny (the idea that God intended for the United States to stretch from the Atlantic to the Pacific) as well as a desire for a better life or perhaps just a little adventure. Of course, as Lubbrage points out, the pioneer's life was very dangerous, including encounters with bandits and hostile Indians. For this reason, the increased number of settlers moving into the western territories required a larger military presence.[5]

The Buffalo Soldiers were created to meet this new demand. With the Civil War over, maintaining a

5

large Union army was no longer practical. From a high of almost a quarter of a million, the army reduced its strength to just over fifty-six thousand.[6] However, the postwar army would have to take charge of security in the South during Reconstruction as well as maintain order along the frontier and guard the U.S.–Mexican border. As William Leckie explains, even though their numbers may have been drastically reduced, their responsibilities were not. As Civil War soldiers returned to civilian life, new recruits were needed. As a result, the first peacetime regiments of African Americans were formed. The use of black soldiers in the Civil War had been controversial, but the one hundred eighty-six thousand[7] blacks who fought for the Union had proven their value. With the end of slavery, African Americans constituted a large pool of readily available labor, and it made sense that the army would target them for recruitment. In addition, as William Katz points out, black men were attracted to these regiments: "In an age that viewed black men as either comic or dangerous, and steadily reduced the decent jobs open to them, army life offered more dignity than almost anything civilian life had to offer."[8] The formation of the regiments, therefore, seemed like the perfect marriage of needs.

Although many African Americans were eager to join, most did not meet the strict requirements of the

6

army. Historian Fairfax Downey explains that pre–Civil War laws against the education of slaves meant most African Americans could not read or write.[9] Even most freedmen from the North had little or no education. Sergeant and company clerk positions, which required reading and writing skills, went unfilled since the army could not find enough suitable candidates. In fact, Congress had originally called for six black regiments to be formed, but these eventually had to be consolidated into four: two cavalry and two infantry. Unlike an army at war, whose primary focus is to win battles, a peacetime army requires a great deal of paperwork. In addition, Leckie notes, since these units would be posted to the frontier, communications between units often took place by means of written orders, making literacy essential. To correct the problem, the army assigned a high number of chaplains to the Buffalo Soldiers to teach the men to read. The wife of Col. Benjamin Grierson, the first commander of the Tenth Cavalry, also helped teach the men and would write letters home to their families for them.[10]

Recruiting white officers also proved difficult. Cooke explains that given the lack of education among black recruits, white officers frequently had to take on additional duties that would normally be carried out by enlisted men. The primary reason for their reluctance, however, was racism. According to

7

Cooke, while some white officers eagerly accepted their new commands, many others turned down promotions because they would not serve with Black soldiers. Most famously, George Custer declined to command the Ninth Cavalry and held out until another cavalry regiment (the Seventh) was formed for him.[11] Cooke writes that a typical notice from the *Army and Navy Journal* read, "A first Lieutenant of Infantry (white) stationed at a very desirable post desires a transfer with an officer of the same grade, on equal terms if in a white regiment; but if in a colored regiment, a reasonable bonus would be expected."[12]

Sadly, the army's supply clerks treated the Buffalo Solders with the same disregard and racial bias. Monroe Lee Billington explains that although they never lacked quality firearms (the Buffalo Soldiers were among the first units to receive Springfield rifles and Gatling guns when they became available),[13] they had to make do with second-rate clothing, food, and horses. Billington writes that other regiments typically were given custom-made silk banners; African American units made their banners from whatever material they could find.[14]

When the regiments finally formed in 1867, the Buffalo Soldiers set out for their postings along the frontier. The Tenth was based in Kansas, while the other groups were spread out in the southwest cor-

8

ner of Texas. Their new homes were underwhelming, to say the least.[15] Leckie writes, "Their stations were among the most lonely and isolated to be found anywhere in the country and mere service at such posts would seem to have called for honorable mention."[16] Fort Concho, an outpost in San Angelo, Texas, earned particular infamy for its miserable state. When the Ninth Cavalry arrived, they found the windows shattered; the porches, roofs, and floors full of holes; and the outhouses in such filthy disrepair that the men refused to use them.[17]

In addition, as Frank Schubert observes, the settlers the black soldiers had been sent to protect did not welcome them. The units stationed in the Southwest, especially in Texas, faced an especially hostile populace:

> The racism in the Southwest [was] apt to be more brutal than [the racism] on the Northern frontier. Racism in western cities, which were conditioned to the presence of some blacks, probably manifested itself in more subtle and varied ways than it did in isolated agricultural regions like those in northern Wyoming.[18]

African Americans could expect to experience seething hostility all over the frontier, but Texas was a far more dangerous environment. William Dobak writes that since the majority of the Buffalo Soldiers

9

had been raised and had worked in the South, the army believed that they would be better suited for the harsh Texas climate than their white counterparts.[19] Apparently, the problem of sending a large number of black soldiers into an area of former slaveholders who had just lost a war did not seem to concern the army's high command. Predictably, Dobak explains, black soldiers faced just as much danger from the civilians they were sent to protect as from the Indians, Mexicans, and bandits they were supposed to be guarding them against. Violence simmered, and often boiled over, whenever the black soldiers and white civilians met.[20] Even so, as William Katz observes, "The Buffalo Soldiers served their country during an age of mounting anti-Negro violence and hostility and, paradoxically, helped bring the white man's law and order to the frontier."[21]

Still, in their first years the Buffalo Soldiers established themselves as some of the most effective soldiers in the army. Historian Sara Massey remarks that in addition to keeping the peace and subduing Indian raiding parties, they helped map and settle large portions of the frontier. For example, during the nine years they were stationed in Texas, the Ninth scouted 34,420 miles of territory and helped lay three hundred and ten miles of new roads and two hundred miles of telegraph wire.[22]

As Leckie explains, in 1876, the Ninth and Tenth

10

Cavalry regiments were transferred to New Mexico and the front lines of the Indian wars. The U. S. Cavalry had been battling with Apaches for almost four decades and were trying to force them onto a bleak reservation at San Carlos, New Mexico. Understandably, Leckie writes, the Apaches were reluctant to submit to a life confined to this dreadful place. The Ninth and Tenth spent the next four years chasing a band of Apaches under command of Chief Victorio. Through countless engagements, the Buffalo Soldiers proved their bravery in battle and gradually wore down Victorio's band. According to Leckie, in 1880, K Troop of the Ninth Cavalry dealt a decisive blow when they drove off an attack on Fort Tularosa. K Troop then chased the Apaches for four hundred miles before launching an assault on Victorio's forces at the Palomas River. Although Victorio escaped, his forces were badly hurt, and Colonel Grierson and the Tenth Cavalry were able to force him across the border into Mexico. Once there, Leckie writes, Mexican troops took advantage of the Apaches' weakened state and wiped out Victorio and most of his followers.[23]

Victorio's defeat was the Buffalo Soldiers' most famous victory but hardly the only action that they saw along the frontier. Billington states that until the close of the nineteenth century the Buffalo Soldiers fought throughout the West in New Mexico,

Arizona, Utah, and Wyoming. They participated in several more campaigns against the Apache, Comanche, Ute, and Sioux Indians, most notably the pursuit of Geronimo and the suppression of the Ghost Dance Campaign of 1891. That campaign culminated, Billington writes, in the Battle of Wounded Knee, a bloody affair in which the U.S. Cavalry slaughtered one hundred and fifty men, women, and children of the Sioux tribe. Although they took no part in the battle, the Ninth Cavalry moved in afterward to help maintain order. Billington points out, however, that the Buffalo Soldiers were never implicated in this or any other atrocity against innocent Native Americans.[24]

As the Indian Wars ended and more and more settlers turned the frontier into civilization, the Buffalo Soldiers turned to a new arena. Cooke writes that the Ninth and Tenth Cavalry were dismounted and deployed in the Spanish-American War. Once again, the Buffalo Soldiers distinguished themselves in several battles, including the Battle of San Juan Hill, in which they stood side by side with Teddy Roosevelt's Rough Riders. By the close of this war, Cooke observes, the Buffalo Soldiers had put in over three decades of distinguished service since their inception in 1866.[25] Jim Salmon explains that the Buffalo Soldiers continued to serve in much quieter duties in the early twentieth century, mostly

12

deployed as guards along the Mexican border. As the United States entered World War I and II, Salmon writes, other African American units were formed, and the original regiments were merged and reorganized, but the spirit of these original groups lives on. According to Salmon, every year the Guadalupe Mountains National Park features an exhibit of artwork depicting the Ninth and Tenth Cavalry, and Texas Parks and Wildlife employees stage a demonstration of the Buffalo Soldiers at Frijole Ranch.[26]

Those serving in the Buffalo Soldiers rarely received praise or promotions from high command because of the racism infecting the army, but the officers who served with them came to respect them as soldiers and as men. Billington notes that commanders like Ben Grierson, Edward Hatch and John "Black Jack" Pershing overcame racial differences and judged their soldiers to be the finest in the army.[27] These officers made sure their men received praise and recognition for their efforts.[28] Although the armed forces would not desegregate for another forty years, the men who served with the Buffalo Soldiers knew their worth, and the African Americans of the Ninth and Tenth Cavalry and Twenty-fourth and Twenty-fifth Infantry regiments took pride in their accomplishments and in the part they played in opening the western frontier.

Sample Chicago Style Research Paper

CMS 32c

13

Notes

Sources listed in order in which they appear in paper. Second and subsequent references to sources include author's last name, abbreviated title, and page number.

1. Frank Schubert, *Black Valor: Buffalo Soldiers and the Medal of Honor, 1870–1898* (Wilmington, DE: Scholarly Resources, 1997), 54.

2. Bill Cooke, *International Museum of the Horse Web Site*, April 21, 2001, http://www.imh.org.

3. Schubert, *Black Valor,* 2.

4. William Katz, *The Black West: A Documentary and Pictorial History of the African American Role in the Westward Expansion of the United States* (New York: Touchstone, 1987), 201.

5. Michael T. Lubbrage, *Revolution to Reconstruction*, March 6, 2003, http://odur.let.rug/nl/~usa/E/manifest/manifxx.htm.

6. William Leckie, *The Buffalo Soldiers: A Narrative of Negro Cavalry in the West* (Norman: University of Oklahoma Press. 1975), 5–6.

7. Cooke, *Horse Web Site.*

8. Katz, *Black West,* 201.

9. Fairfax Downey, *The Buffalo Soldiers in the Indian Wars* (New York: McGraw-Hill, 1969), 28.

10. Leckie, *Buffalo Soldiers,* 9.

11. Cooke, *Horse Web Site.*

Use *Ibid.* for subsequent references to the same work when there are no intervening references.

12. Ibid.

13. Monroe Lee Billington, "Buffalo Soldiers in the American West, 1896–1898," in *African Americans on the Western Frontier*, eds. Monroe Lee Billington and Roger Hadaway (Boulder: University of Colorado Press), 67.

14

14. Ibid., 67.

15. Leckie, *Buffalo Soldiers,* 17.

16. Ibid., 17.

17. Ibid., 17.

18. Frank Schubert, "Black Soldiers on the White Frontier: Some Factors Influencing Race Relations," *Phylon* 32, no. 4 (1971): 410–15; *JSTOR,* Gale, 415.

19. William Dobak, "Black Regulars on the Frontier," *Wild West* (April 2003): 42–53; *Proquest,* Gale, 44.

20. Schubert, "Black Soldiers," 415.

21. Katz, *Black West,* 202.

22. Sara Massey, *Black Cowboys of Texas* (College Station: Texas A&M University Press, 2000), 87.

23. Leckie, *Buffalo Soldiers,* 228.

24. Billington, "Buffalo Soldiers," 61.

25. Cooke, *Horse Web Site.*

26. Jim Salmon, *American.net Web Site on African Americans in the Armed Services,* 1996, http://www.buffalosoldiers.com.

27. Billington, "Buffalo Soldiers," 69.

28. Ibid., 69.

Entries are listed alpha-
betically according to
author's last name

15

← Center
← Double-
space

Bibliography

Billington, Monroe Lee. "Buffalo Soldiers in the American West, 1896–1898." In *African Americans on the Western Frontier*, edited by Monroe Lee Billington and Roger Hadaway. Boulder: University of Colorado Press, 1998.

Cooke, Bill. *International Museum of the Horse Web Site*. 2001. http://www.imh.org.

Dobak, William. "Black Regulars on the Frontier," *Wild West* (April 2003): 44. *Proquest*, Gale (2003).

Downey, Fairfax. *The Buffalo Soldiers in the Indian Wars*. New York: McGraw-Hill, 1969.

Katz, William L. *The Black West: A Documentary and Pictorial History of the African American Role in the Westward Expansion of the United States.* New York: Touchstone, 1987.

Leckie, William. *The Buffalo Soldiers: A Narrative of Negro Cavalry in the West*. Norman: University of Oklahoma Press, 1975.

Lubbrage, Michael T. *Revolution to Reconstruction*. March 6, 2003. http://odur.let.rug.nl/~usa/E/manifest/manifxx.htm.

Massey, Sara. *Black Cowboys of Texas*. College Station: Texas A&M University Press, 2000.

Mississippi State University. *Buffalo Soldiers*. December 16, 1997. http://members.tripod.com/~buffalos/Photo_Gallery.htm.

Salmon, Jim. *American.net Web Site on African Americans in the Armed Services*. 1996. http://www.buffalosoldiers.com.

Schubert, Frank. "Black Soldiers on the White Frontier: Some Factors Influencing Race Relations." *Phylon* 32, no. 4 (1971): 410. *JSTOR,* Gale (2003).

———. *Black Valor: Buffalo Soldiers and the Medal of Honor, 1870–1898*. Wilmington, DE: Scholarly Resources, 1997.

First line of each entry is flush with left-hand margin; subsequent lines indented ¼ inch

Article has no listed author; alphabetized according to first significant word of title

201

CHAPTER 33

ADDITIONAL WRITING MODELS

This chapter explains and illustrates four assignments commonly given in history courses: the lecture review, the book review, the prospectus, and the annotated bibliography.

33a Assignment 1: Lecture Review

Attend three lectures by noted historians who will visit campus this semester. For each lecture, write a lecture review in which you evaluate the information you gained during that lecture and explain how that information adds to what you have learned in this course.

Be critical in this review by making certain not to just summarize what the lecturer said. Was it useful? Did the lecturer support his or her claims adequately? If not, what more could he or she have done to support those claims? Overall, was the lecture worth your time and the department's money?

SAMPLE LECTURE REVIEW

Lecture: "The Last Daughter of Davis Ridge"

Melinda James

HIST 3005

Dr. Cecelski

26 February 2003

SAMPLE LECTURE REVIEW

Review 2

David Cecelski's lecture on the population of slave watermen on Davis Ridge and along other parts of the Atlantic Coast addressed the problems of racism and slavery and presented historical analysis of the coastal antebellum and Jim Crow periods. The lecture was both enlightening and thoughtful, as it raised issues regarding black and white relations in remote areas of the coast. It also contrasted these harmonious relationships with those that existed on the mainland, which was sometimes a mere twenty miles or so away.

Several key points stood out in the lecture. Cecelski analyzed racial attitudes on the coast between whites and blacks during the pre–Civil War, Civil War, and Jim Crow periods. Cecelski noted that even during the height of segregation and oppression under Jim Crow laws, a period which to many was looked upon as a time of discrimination worse that that seen before and during the Civil War, whites and blacks coexisted on Davis Ridge, where they worked together, dined together, and retained close friendships with one another. On Davis Ridge, said Cecelski, the color of one's skin was not judged, but rather what was judged were one's abilities and one's character. While this may sound like a premonition of Martin Luther King Jr.'s "dream," it was rather a wonderful example of a nonstereotypical southern community that employed blacks as well as whites to do what needed to be done.

Perhaps the influences of the coastal environment and the need for good workers played a role in this seemingly "multiracial nirvana." Cecelski also pointed out

SAMPLE LECTURE REVIEW

Review 3

that during the antebellum years, many slaves worked on the coast, fishing for their masters and in many cases even captaining boats. These skills would prove useful in the postwar years and probably relieved racial tensions almost by necessity. After all, as Cecelski stated, when the work needed to be done, racial barriers were immediately removed. Not only were racial barriers absent but social ones as well. There was no room for leaders; instead, individuals all worked for the good of the community and for each other. In order to put food on the table, everyone had to work together and work equally.

Another interesting part of the lecture contrasted the treatment of minorities on Davis Ridge and in other coastal areas with that of those on the mainland. As the Klu Klux Klan marched in larger coastal towns like New Bern, people on the barrier islands of North Carolina felt little impact of their presence. While a black man on the streets of New Bern might not survive after dark due to race-related violence, a black man in a coastal community like Davis Ridge did not need to worry about such dangers, at least not to the same extent.

Another interesting point Cecelski made was the importance of oral history. In order to learn about Davis Ridge, he had to obtain information from people who actually grew up there. When he began his research, no survivors of Davis Ridge remained. The bulk of his findings were contained in an interview with Nanny Ward, an elderly black woman born in 1911, by two other historians. The interview had been conducted with her in

SAMPLE LECTURE REVIEW

Review 4

the early 1990s and focused on her growing up on Davis Ridge during the era of Jim Crow laws. If not for this interview, which consisted of her simply remembering intimate details of coastal life in the past, no substantial history of Davis Ridge would have remained, nor would it have ever been recorded.

Although I always knew of the importance of oral history, I always took for granted that if I ever wanted to know anything about the history of our state, or about any state or region in this country or abroad, I could always find it online or printed in a book. Oral history has always fascinated me, but I don't think I ever fully appreciated its relevance to the understanding of our past until this lecture. Cecelski made me realize how vital the memories of our elderly are to our study of days gone by. He made me realize that once these kind, gentle folk have died, their memories pass with them. And without their recollections, memories, and stories being passed on to our generation and beyond, we may never fully understand life in remote areas of the world, such as Davis Ridge on North Carolina's barrier islands.

Dr. Cecelski's lecture gave me an insightful and thoughtful look into the interpersonal relationships and lives of blacks and whites under Jim Crow laws and showed me how coastal areas like Davis Ridge differed from other Southern port cities.

Davis Ridge was almost totally wiped off the map in a massive twentieth-century hurricane. Although it had virtually ceased to exist during her interview, Nanny Ward still spoke of how she wished she could go back there one last time.

Assignment 2: Book Review

The major assignments in this course are reviews of three important books concerning American history since 1877. Keep in mind that a book review is more than a summary: you must analyze and evaluate the book. For example, you must evaluate the author's thesis as well as its style and content. Is he or she persuasive? Is this a good book? Why or why not? What are the book's major strengths and weaknesses? What types of sources did the author use?

SAMPLE BOOK REVIEW

Robert Darnton's *The Great Cat Massacre*

Josh Hasty

History 301

Dr. Swanson

30 September 2003

SAMPLE BOOK REVIEW

The Great Cat Massacre 2

First published in 1985, Robert Darnton's *The Great Cat Massacre* attempts to bring to light many of the historically substantial cultural events of eighteenth-century France. As the author describes the book's intention, the book "investigates ways of thinking in eighteenth-century France."[1] The author, for the most part, succeeds in his goal of passing on to the reader this knowledge of odd cultural happenings during the Old Regime. The intended audience for this book seems to be somewhat mainstream readers, not professional historians, though it seems that scholars have also found value in the work because it has been mentioned in a number of scholarly journals.

The book is divided into six chapters, each of which is essentially an essay devoted to the specifics of either an eighteenth-century French cultural event or a common practice of the period, such as the telling of folk stories. Since the book was written less than twenty years ago, the views expressed in it have not changed drastically. Darnton's opinions of the selected events contained within the text would seem to be as influential today as they were when the book was first published. Much of the book is written in a narrative style though the book is mostly a description of events accompanied by the author's observations on subjects.

The book deals with a variety of fascinating subjects. Special attention is given in one section of the book to the folk tradition of passing along what we now call fairy

The Great Cat Massacre 3

tales. Familiar children's stories like "Little Red Riding Hood" and "Cinderella," which were originally passed along among those in the peasant class in eighteenth-century Europe, are revealed to have existed in very different forms from those we know today. "Little Red Riding Hood," for example, had a very different meaning depending on where one heard it (the original French version differs from other versions throughout Europe, for example). Darnton mentions references to violence, innocence, and virginity, which were present on many levels in the story's original form, in which the wolf eats the grandmother, has the young girl strip naked and join him in bed and then devours her.[2] This trend continues throughout many stories that have taken on newer, more innocent form in the present day, including "Hansel and Gretel," "Puss n' Boots," and "Sleeping Beauty."

One of the most notable essays in the book is the title essay about what has been labeled the great cat massacre. Here Darnton explains how cats were viewed in eighteenth-century Europe as tools of witches and of the devil himself and as symbols of sex (an association that continues today throughout the Western world). Because of these and many other negative connotations attributed to cats, a group of workers who felt they had been treated a step below that of their mistress's cat took advantage of their master's order to rid the grounds of stray cats by capturing every cat in sight (including the mistress's personal pet). They held a mock trial for these

SAMPLE BOOK REVIEW

The Great Cat Massacre 4

cats and, after finding every one of them guilty, hanged them on makeshift gallows. The workers were alleged to have then laughed about the incident for weeks.[3]

As Darnton points out, in our modern day it is hard to fathom the joy these workers found in the slaying of defenseless animals. What lies below the surface, however, is the association that cats had with the bourgeois class in general and with their spiteful mistress in particular. By slaying the stray cats (along with the mistress's beloved *Le Gris,* which they surely enjoyed killing most of all), the working class was striking back at the upper class in one of the few ways they could: in effigy. In addition, by capturing and killing *Le Gris,* the workers were essentially calling their mistress a witch; by killing her cat, they were suggesting that they would in fact like to kill her. It is difficult for modern-day citizens of the Western world to accept this behavior, but when viewed in the context of the workers' situation and beliefs, it is possible to understand why the great cat massacre took place.

Another example of understanding the views of eighteenth-century France comes in the form of an anonymous middle-class citizen's intricate "description" (for lack of a better term) of Montpellier as it was in his time. Darnton expresses that we do not know exactly why this anonymous author crafted this exquisite, yet lacking (in terms of a literary standpoint) view of the city. Further, we as modern-day readers have a difficult time

SAMPLE BOOK REVIEW

The Great Cat Massacre 5

maintaining a firm grip on the picture the author is trying to paint for us. We do not know exactly how Montpellier looked in 1768 when the author was describing it, and he unfortunately did not seem to be writing to give future generations a clear picture of the city, now forever lost in the form in which it was described.[4] This leaves the modern-day reader with the task of trying to make sense of it all, a task which more often than not proves frustrating as the piece seems to have been written as a tribute to the city of Montpellier in 1768, not as a historical record to be referred to by future historians.

Darton describes a time when literary activity was sharply curtailed by the authorities. In his fourth essay, he describes a police inspector of the period, Joseph D'Hemery, who kept detailed files of writers and philosophers the government was "keeping an eye on." Many writers of the period were arrested for writing unfavorably of the government or religion, and this is documented in the policeman's files. These many files contained D'Hemery personal opinion on each writer's work or samples of the writing itself. D'Hemery often kept tabs on writers' contacts, and this occasionally included keeping watch on wives and children.[5] This essay not only illustrates eigthteenth-century attitudes towards freedom of expression but also provides a fascinating story of a policeman who also became something of a literary critic.

SAMPLE BOOK REVIEW

The Great Cat Massacre 6

One writer's work that the police were closely following was that of Denis Diderot, who was responsible for publishing encyclopedias. Of this work, D'Hemery wrote, "Its seventeen folio volumes of text include such a jumble of information on everything from A to Z that one cannot help wondering why it raised such a storm in the eighteenth century."[6] Of course, this was not the first reference collection of its time; many dictionaries preceded Diderot's work. Darnton explains the upheaval this way: The knowledge that was expressed in Diderot's work was translated as power; in other words, the categorization of things was seen to be taking too many liberties with the way things were. To say that one thing is this kind of animal (a squirrel being a rodent, for example) and another is a different animal (a Great Dane being a dog) was seen by many to be a proclamation of the way things were to be.[7] Once again, it is difficult now to see how this could be interpreted as a horrible injustice. We now live in a time when things have been classified for us. We know what a squirrel is and what a dog is, but during eighteenth-century Europe, says Darnton, many such things were in dispute, and to declare things one way or another was to display a great deal of influence and power over the masses. This is a real-world example of knowledge being associated with power.

Darnton's final essay involves what he refers to as the mystery of reading:

What in fact was reading in eighteenth-century

The Great Cat Massacre 7

France? Reading still remains a mystery, although we do it every day. The experience is so familiar that it seems perfectly comprehensible. But if we could really comprehend it, if we could understand how we construe meaning from little figures printed on a page, we could begin to penetrate the deeper mystery of how people orient themselves in the world of symbols spun around them by their culture.[8]

This seems to be the most difficult—and, at a casual glance, the most absurd—question the book raises. The essay attempts to unravel the meaning of reading in the eighteenth century (mostly of Rousseau and similar philosophers) and perhaps the meaning of reading today as well. Darnton follows the reading habits of Jean Ranson, a merchant in eighteenth-century France, noting the demographics of the target audience for books and how those like Ranson "digested" books but never quite comes up with a definitive answer. This essay is for the most part simply a study of what one middle-class man read; it does not answer the question of how an eighteenth-century European read or make sense of the symbols that Darnton speaks of earlier in the piece. This is the only essay in the book that seems to leave the reader without an answer to the author's question (though the essay remains intriguing in and of itself).

Several reviews of this book have appeared in scholarly journals. Most identify the fascinating yet pop-

The Great Cat Massacre 8

culture-like tone of the book. For example, Phillip Stewart writes of the title of the book: "The [Workers Revolt Essay], incidentally, is the chapter dealing with the great cat massacre, which as far as one can tell is featured on the title page only because it is catchy. As this suggests, the somewhat popularizing tone may appeal more to the casual reader than to the specialist."[9] David E. Apter, another reviewer, sees Darnton's narrow view of daily life in eighteenth-century Europe as a positive addition to other scholarly works on the subject: "Darnton is concerned with daily life as seen from below, where history remains largely unwritten. His technique is different from historical sociology. For him, history is reconstructed as narrative and text. Settings of life convey meaning through events used as metaphors and metonymies. . . . [Social networks and codes] are revealed in individual histories."[10]

When considering these two quite opposite reviews, one must remain mindful that the first is from a historical journal, *Eighteenth Century Studies* and the second, which contains more praise for the work, is from the *American Journal of Sociology.* Both reviews are equally important in their own right, and they both convey views of American scholars during the last twenty years; they also convey the views from two different scholarly fields. A historian is more concerned with how people affected certain events. A sociologist, on the other hand, is more concerned with how certain events affected people.

The Great Cat Massacre 9

These contrasting perspectives put the two opinions of the book in perspective and lead the reader to believe, based on its focus on individuals and social groups, that perhaps this book is more a sociological study of the eighteenth century than a historical study.

The author is clearly a product of the last twenty years. Though views have changed somewhat, most of Darnton's views (for example, that killing cats and persecuting writers are not acceptable today) would seem to remain the same. Darnton is a historian first and foremost, and though it may seem at times that he addresses a sociological audience, the book was, so far as the reader can tell, written for a historical audience. As for Darnton's writing style, it has been accused of being contrary to that of the *Annales* school of thinking. Roger Chartier, a noted *Annales* scholar, has said that Darnton has not conveyed a "fair expression of what French historians are producing today."[11] Perhaps this is due to the sociological spin that Darnton gives the essays in *The Great Cat Massacre*.

In the end, the book is a solid study of everyday life in eighteenth-century France. Just about every social class is represented, from peasants to bourgeois, and the intricacies of their views are all well communicated. It would seem that this was the very reason the book was written—to try to bring the reader closer to culture in eighteenth-century France. The book does not necessarily give readers any final answers. In fact, as Darnton writes

SAMPLE BOOK REVIEW

The Great Cat Massacre 10

in his conclusion, "I doubt that any of us will come up with the final answers. The questions keep changing, and the history never stops."[12]

SAMPLE BOOK REVIEW

The Great Cat Massacre 11

Notes

1. Robert Darnton, *The Great Cat Massacre and Other Episodes in French Cultural History* (New York: Vintage, 1985), 3.

2. Darnton, *Great Cat Massacre,* 11.

3. Ibid., 75–77.

4. Ibid., 107.

5. Ibid., 170.

6. Ibid., 192.

7. Ibid., 192–193.

9. Phillip Stewart, "The Great Cat Massacre and Other Episodes in French Cultural History," *Eighteenth-Century Studies* 19, no. 2 (Winter 1985–1986), 260.

10. David E. Apter, "The Great Cat Massacre and Other Episodes in French Cultural History," *American Journal of Sociology* 91, no. 3 (November 1985), 695–96.

11. Dominick LaCapra, "Chartier, Darnton, and the Great Symbol Massacre," *Journal of Modern History* 60, no. 1 (March 1988), 96.

12. Darnton, *Great Cat Massacre,* 263.

SAMPLE BOOK REVIEW

The Great Cat Massacre 12

Bibliography

Apter, David E. "The Great Cat Massacre and Other
Episodes in French Cultural History." *American Journal
of Sociology* 91, no. 3 (November 1985): 695–96.

Darnton, Robert, *The Great Cat Massacre and Other
Episodes in French Cultural History*. New York:
Vintage, 1985.

LaCapra, Dominick. "Charter, Darnton, and the Great
Symbol Massacre." *Journal of Modern History* 60,
no. 1 (March 1988):96.

Stewart, Philip. "The Great Cat Massacre and Other
Episodes in French Cultural History." *Eighteenth-
Century Studies* 19, no. 2 (Winter 1985–1986): 260.

33c Assignment Three: Prospectus

Prior to writing a research paper, you will need to have your topic approved. To do so, you will be required to write a prospectus in which you identify the subject you plan to write about, the questions you intend to answer, and the sources you will use.

SAMPLE PROSPECTUS

Prospectus for Historiography on Reconstruction

Jen Sierra

HIST 3000

Dr. Parkerson

31 August 2003

SAMPLE PROSPECTUS

Reconstruction 2

In my paper, I plan to address the topic of Reconstruction from several angles, including an investigation of Andrew Johnson's role in Reconstruction after Lincoln's assassination.

Howard K. Beale's *The Critical Year: A Study of Andrew Johnson and Reconstruction* is a balanced source that can provide an overview of the topic. To address the Southern concerns about and arguments against Reconstruction, specifically the problem of Northern economic interests, Claude G. Bowers's *The Tragic Era: The Revolution After Lincoln* provides a southern perspective. Finally, as a counterpoint to Bowers, Kenneth M. Stampp's *The Era of Reconstruction* illustrates a revisionist view to W. E. Be. Du Bois' ideas expressed in earlier historical texts. Some supplemental material may be drawn from James M. McPherson's *Battle Cry of Freedom,* a much broader source that deals with many political and social aspects of the Civil War as well as Reconstruction.

Though there are many parts of Reconstruction that will not be given direct attention in this historiography, I hope to bring as much diversity as possible to the subject by consulting these sources. My three most important sources are listed, with full source information, on the next page.

SAMPLE PROSPECTUS

Reconstruction 3

Bibliography

Beale, Howard K. *The Critical Year: A Study of Andrew Johnson and Reconstruction.* New York: Unger, 1958.

Bowers, Claude G. *The Tragic Era: The Revolution after Lincoln.* New York: Halcyon, 1929.

Stampp, Kenneth M. *The Era of Reconstruction.* New York: Knopf, 1965.

33d Assignment Four: Annotated Bibliography

In preparation for writing a fifteen- to twenty-page research paper, you are to submit an annotated bibliography of six to eight sources that you will rely upon in your paper. In this bibliography, you must briefly but accurately summarize what each book has to offer you as you conduct research for your paper.

SAMPLE ANNOTATED BIBLIOGRAPHY

Annotated Bibliography

Todd Connor

Hist 3000

Dr. Parkerson

23 August 2002

SAMPLE ANNOTATED BIBLIOGRAPHY

Annotated Bibliography 2

Chambers, John Whiteclay II, and G. Kurt Piehler, eds. *Major Problems in American Military History.* Boston: Houghton Mifflin, 1999. This is a collection of essays and other documents about specific problems in military history during various time periods. This source is valuable because it includes a number of first-person narratives from troops on the front lines during America's many conflicts.

Degregorio, William A. *Complete Book of U. S.Presidents.* 5th ed. New York: Barricade, 1996. This book surveys U. S. presidents by providing detailed information on each president ranging from George Washington to Bill Clinton.

Foner, Eric. *Reconstruction: America's Unfinished Revolution.* New York: Harper & Row, 1988. This is one of the leading texts on the period of Reconstruction. The author focuses specifically on the state of the Union following the Civil War.

Foote, Shelby. *The Civil War: A Narrative: Fort Sumter to Perryville.* New York: Vintage, 1958. This book is the first volume of the author's series on the Civil War. It is presented in a narrative style.

McPherson, James M. *Battle Cry of Freedom: The Civil War Era.* New York: Ballantine, 1988. This book is a single-volume history encompassing the entire Civil War era. The author describes with precise detail the period of the 1850s through the beginning of Reconstruction.

SAMPLE ANNOTATED BIBLIOGRAPHY

Annotated Bibliography 3

Millett, Allan R., and Peter Maslowski. *For the Common Defense: A Military History of the United States of America.* New York: Free Press, 1984. This work provides a broad survey of U. S. military history.

Perman, Michael, ed. *Major Problems in the Civil War and Reconstruction.* Boston: Houghton Mifflin, 1998. This book offers a collection of documents and essays written about and during the Civil War. Essays and letters written by both civilians and soldiers on both sides are represented.

PART 8

PRACTICAL WRITING

CHAPTER 34
DESIGNING DOCUMENTS AND WEB PAGES

CHAPTER 35
WRITING FOR THE WORKPLACE

CHAPTER 36
MAKING ORAL PRESENTATIONS

CHAPTER 34

DESIGNING DOCUMENTS AND WEB PAGES

This chapter presents general guidelines for designing documents (papers, letters, reports, and so on) and Web pages, as well as specific advice for making all your papers easier to read.

34a Understanding Document Design

Document design refers to the conventions that determine the way a document—a research paper, memo, report, business letter, or résumé, for example—looks on a page. In general, well-designed documents have the following characteristics:

- An effective format
- Clear subheadings
- Useful lists
- Attractive visuals

(1) Creating an Effective Format

Margins Your document should have at least a one-inch margin on all sides.

Line Spacing Line spacing refers to the amount of space between the lines of a document. All copy must be double-spaced or triple-spaced. The rule about double-spacing applies not only to the text but also to block quotations and case histories within the text, to notes, to appendix material, to bibliographies and indexes—that is, to *all* parts of the manuscript.

Font Size To create a readable document, use a 10- or 12-point font. Avoid fonts that will distract readers (script or cursive fonts, for example).

White Space You can use white space around a block of text—a paragraph or a section, for example—to focus readers' attention on the material you are isolating.

(2) Using Subheadings

Subheadings tell readers what to expect in a section before they actually read it. In addition, because they break up a text, subheadings make a document inviting and easy to read.

Number of Subheadings The number of subheadings depends on the document. A long, complicated document will need more subheadings than a shorter, less complex one. Keep in mind that too few subheadings may not be of much use, but too many subheadings will make your document look like an outline.

See 12a *Phrasing* Subheadings can also be phrases (always stated in **parallel** terms, as in the following examples): *The Preconditions of History, The Political Crisis, The First Battle of Bull Run.* They can also be questions (*What Is An Incomplete Historian?*) or statements (*Theory Has Its Limitations*).

Placement Subheadings of different levels may be differentiated in a manuscript by their placement on the page. The first-level subhead, for example, may be centered; the second-level subhead may be keyed flush left; a third-level subhead may then be indented a few spaces or it may be run in at the beginning of a paragraph and end with a period. No period follows a subhead typed on a line by itself.

Typographical Emphasis You can emphasize subheadings by using **boldface,** *italics,* or ALL CAPITAL LETTERS. Used in moderation, these distinctive typefaces make a text more readable. Used excessively, however, they slow readers down.

(3) Constructing Lists

A list makes material easier to understand by breaking complicated statements into a series of key ideas. Lists are easiest to read when all the elements are parallel and about the same length. When rank is important, number the items in the list; when it isn't, use **bullets** (as in the list below). Make sure you introduce the list with a complete sentence followed by a colon.

We must examine the contributions of several individuals when we consider the outcome of the Civil War:
- How George McClellan led the Army of the Potomac
- The way General Pope fared at Second Bull Run
- Why Jeb Stuart entered the Chambersburg Raid

Because the items on the list above are not complete sentences, they do not end with periods. If the items on a list are sentences, end each with a period.

(4) Creating Effective Visuals

Visuals, such as tables, graphs, diagrams, and photographs, can enhance your documents. You can create your own tables and graphs by using a computer program such as *Excel, Lotus,* or *Microsoft Word.* In addition, you can get diagrams and photographs by photocopying or scanning them from a print source or by downloading them from the Internet or from CD-ROMs or DVDs. Remember, however, that if you use a visual from a source, you must supply appropriate See Pt. 7 **documentation**.

Tables Tables present data in a condensed visual format—arranged in rows and columns. Tables most often present numerical data, although occasionally they include words as well as numbers. Keep in mind that tables may distract readers, so include only those that are necessary to support your discussion. The following table reports the writer's original research and therefore needs no documentation.

Crane 8

Table 1 shows that the number of students studying maritime history has grown since 1990 and is now greater than the number of students in the traditional history curriculum.

Heading

Table 1. Number of history students in maritime history vs. traditional curriculum at East Carolina University, 1990–1997

Descriptive caption

Year	Maritime history	Traditional curriculum
1990	3	64
1991	5	66
1992	12	54
1993	14	33
1994	15	30
1995	17	29
1996	29	16
1997	32	23

Data

This trend seems to be consistent with patterns across the country where maritime history is an option in undergraduate history curricula.

Graphs Whereas tables present specific numerical data, graphs convey the general pattern or trend that the data suggest. Because graphs tend to be more general (and therefore less accurate) than tables, they are frequently accompanied by tables. The following is an example of a bar graph reproduced from a source.

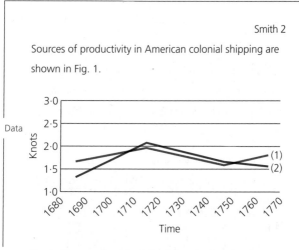

Smith 2

Sources of productivity in American colonial shipping are shown in Fig. 1.

Data

Label and descriptive caption

Credit line

Fig. 1. Sources of productivity change in American colonial shipping, 1675–1775. (Reproduced by permission from Gary M. Walton, "Sources of Productivity Change in American Colonial Shipping, 1675–1775," *Economic History Review* 10 [1967]: 67–78.)

Very little change took place during this one hundred-year period.

Understanding Document Design

Diagrams   A diagram enables you to focus on specific details of a mechanism or object. Diagrams are often used in scientific and technical writing to clarify concepts while eliminating the need for paragraphs of detailed and confusing description.

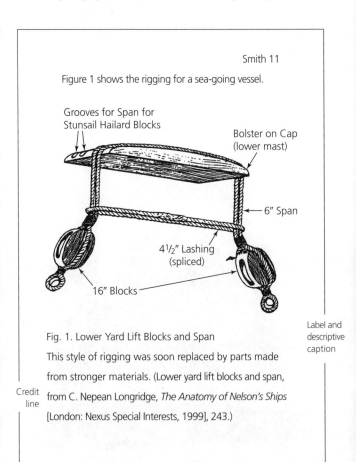

Smith 11

Figure 1 shows the rigging for a sea-going vessel.

Grooves for Span for
Stunsail Hailard Blocks

Bolster on Cap
(lower mast)

6″ Span

4½″ Lashing
(spliced)

16″ Blocks

Label and
descriptive
caption

Fig. 1. Lower Yard Lift Blocks and Span

This style of rigging was soon replaced by parts made

from stronger materials. (Lower yard lift blocks and span,

Credit
line

from C. Nepean Longridge, *The Anatomy of Nelson's Ships*

[London: Nexus Special Interests, 1999], 243.)

Photographs Photographs enable you to show exactly what something or someone looks like—an animal in its natural habitat, a work of fine art, or an actor in costume, for example. Although computer technology that enables you to paste photographs directly into a text is widely available, you should use it with restraint. Not every photograph will support or enhance your written text; in fact, an irrelevant photograph will distract readers.

Jones 9

Sailors took known risks by sailing with Nelson. In a typical sailing ship of the time (see Fig. 2), . . .

Label and descriptive caption   Fig. 2. One view of a typical ship (The Granger Collection)

Credit line

Many sailors aboard such vessels . . .

☑ CHECKLIST: INCLUDING VISUALS IN THE TEXT

✔ Use a visual only when it contributes something important to the discussion, not for embellishment.

✔ Include the visual in the text only if you plan to discuss it in your paper (place the visual in an appendix if you do not).

✔ Introduce each visual with a complete sentence.

✔ Follow each visual with a discussion of its significance.

✔ Leave wide margins around each visual.

✔ Place each visual as close as possible to the section of your document in which it is discussed.

✔ Label each visual appropriately.

✔ Determine whether a borrowed visual falls under the **fair use doctrine**.

✔ Include a credit line that documents each visual that is borrowed from a source.

See 34b1

34b Designing Web Pages

Because many colleges and universities provide students with a full range of Internet services, you may have the opportunity to create a Web page—or even a full Web site. Like other documents, Web pages are subject to specific conventions of document design.

The easiest way to create a Web page is to use one of the many Web creation software packages that are commercially available. These programs automatically convert text and graphics into HTML (the programming language by which standard documents are converted into World Wide Web hypertext documents) so that they can be posted on the Web.

(1) Building a Web Site

A personal **home page** usually contains information about how to contact the author, a brief biography, and links to other Web sites. A home page can be expanded into a full **Web site** (a group of related Web pages). Basic Web pages contain only text, but more advanced Web pages include photographs, animation, and even film clips. You can get ideas for your Web page by examining other Web pages and determining what appeals to you. Keep in mind, however, that although you may borrow formatting ideas from a Web site, it is never acceptable to appropriate a site's content.

WEB SITES AND COPYRIGHT

As a rule, you should assume that any material on the Web is copyrighted unless the author makes an explicit statement to the contrary. This means that you must receive written permission if you are going to reproduce this material on your Web site. The only exception to this rule is the **fair use doctrine,** which allows the use of copyrighted material for the purpose of commentary, parody, or research and education. How much of the work you use is also of consideration, and so is the purpose of your use—whether or not you are using it commercially. Thus you can quote a sentence of an article from the *New York Times* for the purpose of commenting on it, but you must get permission from the *New York Times* to reproduce the article in its entirety on your Web site. As of now, you do not, however, have to get permission to provide a link to the article on the *New York Times's* Web site. (Material you quote in a research paper for one of your classes falls under the fair use doctrine and does not require permission.)

(2) Organizing Information

Before creating a Web site, sketch a basic plan on a piece of paper. Consider how your Web pages will be connected and what links you will provide to other Web sites. Your home page should provide an overview of your site and give readers a clear sense of what material the site will contain. Beginning with the home page, users will navigate from one piece of information to another.

As you plan your Web site, consider how your pages will be organized. If your site is relatively uncomplicated, you can arrange pages so that one page leads sequentially to the next. If your site is relatively complicated, however, you will have to group pages in order of their importance or of their relevance to a particular category. The home page of the *Pocket Handbook's* Web site, for example, indicates that information is grouped under various headings—Learning Resources, Review, and Online Writing Centers, for example (see Figure 1).

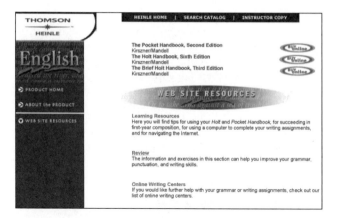

Figure 1 *Home page of* The Pocket Handbook's *Web site*

(3) Designing a Web Site

When you design your Web site, lay out text and graphics so that they present your ideas clearly and logically. Because your home page is the first thing readers will encounter, it should be clear and easy to follow. Present related items next to each other, and use text sparingly. Make sure you identify items on the same topic by highlighting them in the same color or by using the same font or graphic. Remember, however, that using too many graphics or fancy type styles will confuse readers.

(4) Providing Links

Your home page will probably include buttons and links. **Buttons**—graphic icons, such as arrows or pictures—enable readers to move from one page of a Web site to another. **Links** (short for hyperlinks)—words or URLs (electronic addresses) highlighted and underlined in blue—enable readers to navigate from one site to another. When you provide a link, you are directing people to the Web site to which the link refers. For this reason, be certain that the site is up and running and that the information that appears there is reliable.

(5) Proofreading Your Text

Before you post your site on the Web, proofread the text of your Web pages just as you would any other document. If you have included links on your Web site, be sure you have entered the full Web address (beginning with http://). If you have used a colored background or text, be sure you have avoided color combinations that make your pages difficult to read (purple on black, for example). Finally, make certain you have received permission to use all material—graphics as well as text—that you have borrowed from a source and that you have documented this material.

(6) Posting Your Web Site

Once you have designed a Web site, you will need to upload, or **post,** it so you can view it on the Web. Most commonly, Web pages are posted with **FTP** (File Transfer Protocol) software.

See 29b4

To get your site up on the Web, you transfer your files to an **Internet server,** a computer that is connected at all times to the Internet. Your Internet service provider will instruct you on how to use FTP to transfer your files. Once your site is up and running, you will instantly be able to see if you have made any mistakes. These errors will be apparent as soon as you view your pages on the Web.

Your next step is to publicize your new Web site. Even though many search engines automatically search for new Web sites, you should give formal notification to them that you have launched a new site. Most search engines have links to pages where you can register new sites (see Figure 2). In addition, you can access Web sites that automatically send your information to a number of different search engines. (By doing this, you avoid having to repeat the same information each time you register. You can find these sites by doing a keyword search of the phrase "site registration.")

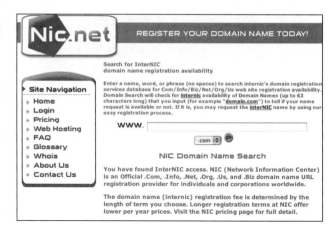

Figure 2 Home page of a registration provider

✅ CHECKLIST: CREATING A WEB SITE

- ✔ Decide what content and design appeal to you.
- ✔ Make sure you do not plagiarize another site's content.
- ✔ Consider how you want your site to be organized.
- ✔ Draw a basic plan of your site.
- ✔ Lay out text and graphics so that they present your ideas clearly and logically.
- ✔ Keep both text and graphics simple.
- ✔ Provide clear and informative links.
- ✔ Proofread your text.
- ✔ Make sure your site looks the way you want it to.
- ✔ Make sure all your links are active.
- ✔ Makes sure you have acknowledged all material that you have borrowed from a source.
- ✔ Post your site to an Internet server.
- ✔ Notify search engines that your site is up and running.

CHAPTER 35

WRITING FOR
THE WORKPLACE

Whether you are writing letters of application, résumés, memos, or e-mail, you should always be concise, avoid digressions, and try to sound as natural as possible.

35a Writing Letters of Application

A letter of application summarizes your qualifications for a particular job. Begin by identifying the job and telling where you heard about it. In the body of your letter, provide the information that will convince readers you are qualified for the position. Conclude by reinforcing your desire for the job and by stating that you have enclosed your résumé.

Single-space within paragraphs and double-space between paragraphs. Proofread carefully to make sure there are no errors in spelling or punctuation. Most business letters use **block** format, with all parts of the letter aligned on the left-hand margin.

SAMPLE LETTER OF APPLICATION: BLOCK FORMAT

26 First Street
Spartanburg, SC 29303
December 17, 2001
Pab1230@seanet.com   Heading

Allen Hahn, Esq.
Hahn, Bryant, and Sims   Inside
114 Butler Avenue   address
North Wales, PA 19454

Dear Mr. Hahn: Salutation

My college advisor, Dr. Ernest Crane, has told me
that you are interested in hiring a paralegal for
summer 2002. I believe that my academic
background and my work experience qualify me
for this position.

I am presently a junior history major at the   Body
University of South Carolina. During the past year,
I have taken courses in international policy,
constitutional law, and the civil rights movement.
I am a careful and accurate researcher, having   ←   Single
served as Dr. Crane's research assistant for the   space
past two semesters. I am proficient in Microsoft
Word, Microsoft PowerPoint, and Excel.   ←   Double
                                                       space
After I graduate, I hope to attend the University
of South Carolina School of Law and then return
to Pennsylvania to practice law. I hope to study
copyright law as it pertains to international policy.
I believe my interest in copyright law may enable
me to make a contribution to your firm even as a
paralegal.

I have enclosed a résumé for your examination. I
will be available for an interview at your
convenience. I look forward to hearing from you.

Sincerely,   Complimentary close

Paul Andrew Bates

Paul Andrew Bates   Typed signature
Enc.: Résumé   Additional data

35b Preparing Résumés

A résumé lists relevant information about your education, job experience, goals, and personal interests. The most common way to arrange the information in your résumé is in chronological order, listing your education and work experience in sequence, moving from earliest to latest. Your résumé should be brief (one page, if possible), clear, and logically organized. Emphasize important information with italics, bullets, boldface, or different fonts. Print your résumé on high-quality paper, and proofread carefully for errors.

SCANNABLE RÉSUMÉS

Although the majority of résumés are submitted on paper, an increasing number of résumés are designed to be scanned into a database. If you submit such a résumé, format it accordingly. Because scanners will not pick up columns, bullets, or italics, you should not use them in a scannable résumé. Whereas in print résumés you use strong action verbs to describe your accomplishments (*conducted research,* for example), in a scannable résumé you use key nouns or adjectives (*careful and accurate researcher,* for example) to attract employers who carry out a keyword search for applicants with certain skills. (To facilitate such a search, you should include a Keyword section at the bottom of your scannable résumé.)

SAMPLE PRINT RÉSUMÉ: EMPHATIC ORDER

PAUL ANDREW BATES

SCHOOL
314 Harding Drive
Columbia, SC 21774
(864) 221-1212

HOME
26 First Street
Spartanburg, SC 29303
(864) 587-3126

LEGAL EXPERIENCE

Hahn, Bryant, and Sims, North Wales, Pa. Paralegal.
Conducted research on copyright law and wrote
summaries. Typed and edited legal briefs. Answered
phones and arranged appointments for Mr. Sims.
Summer 2002.

University of South Carolina, Columbia, S.C.
Research Assistant.
Assisted Dr. Ernest Crane in research for his book,
International Law and U.S. Copyright. Summarized
key articles. Spring and fall semesters 2001.

OTHER WORK EXPERIENCE

King Memorial Library, Spartanburg, S.C. Circulation
Assistant.
Checked out, filed, shelved, and catalogued books.
Summers 2000, 2001, and 2002.

EDUCATION

University of South Carolina, Columbia, S.C. (senior)
History major. Expected date of graduation:
May 2003.
Greenville County High School, Spartanburg, S.C.

INTERESTS

Member South Carolina Students of History
Member of University Chess Club

REFERENCES

Charles Sims, Esq.
Hahn, Bryant, and Simms
114 Butler Avenue
North Wales, Pa. 19454

Dr. Ernest Crane, Professor
Department of History
University of South Carolina
Columbia, S.C. 21774

Mr. Ryan Danahy, Librarian
King Memorial Library
468 Abner Road
Spartanburg, S.C. 29303

SAMPLE RÉSUMÉ: SCANNABLE

PAUL ANDREW BATES

26 First Street   Phone: (864) 587-3126
Spartanburg, SC 29303   E-mail: pab1230@seanet.com

Employment Objective: Entry-level position in a legal firm that will enable me to use my academic knowledge and the skills that I learned in my work experience.

EDUCATION:

University of South Carolina, Bachelor of Arts in History. May 2003. Concentration: History of Copyright Law. Graduated Magna Cum Laude. Overall GPA: 3.755 on a 4.0 base.

SCHOLASTIC HONORS AND AWARDS:

Member of Phi Kappa Phi, Golden Key National Honor Society, College Republicans, and Law Society

EMPLOYMENT EXPERIENCE:

Hahn, Bryant, and Sims, North Wales, Pa., June 2003 to Sept. 2003. Paralegal.
Conducted research on copyright law and wrote summaries. Typed and edited legal briefs. Answered phones and arranged appointments for Mr. Sims.

University of South Carolina, Columbia, S.C., Jan.–May 2001 and Sept.–Dec. Research Assistant. Assisted Dr. Ernest Crane in research for his book, *International Law and U.S. Copyright.* Summarized key articles.

KEY WORDS:

Law. Leadership. Copyright. International policy. Written and oral communication skills. Microsoft Word. Microsoft PowerPoint. Excel.

35c Writing Memos

Memos communicate information within an organization. A memo can be short or long, depending on its purpose. Begin your memo with a purpose statement that presents your reason for writing the memo. Follow this statement with a summary section that tells readers what to expect in the rest of the memo. Then, in the body of your memo, present your support: the detailed information that supports the main point of your memo. If your memo is short, use numbered or bulleted lists to emphasize information. If it is long, use headings to designate the various parts of the memo (*Summary, Background, Benefits,* and so on). End your memo with a statement of your conclusions and recommendations.

SAMPLE MEMO

TO: Gary Lowe, University Attorney
Opening FROM: Kristie Smith, President, Law Club
compo- SUBJECT: Use of Peer Attorneys
nent DATE: November 21, 2002

This memo proposes the establishment of a peer
Purpose attorney system to defend students charged with
statement minor conduct violations on campus.

BACKGROUND
Under the current system, students in residence
halls are required to defend themselves if they
have been accused of violating policies related to
student conduct. Often, however, students are uncomfortable speaking in a student court situation
and do not adequately defend themselves.

NEW POLICY
I propose that we establish a peer attorney program through which members of the Law Club
Body would voulnteer to assist students accused of
minor conduct violations (at no expense to the de-
fendant).

BENEFITS
The benefits of this service would be two-fold.
First, students who have been charged with a
minor offense will have an interested party to turn
to when they prepare their defense. Second, students who, through their involvement in Law Club,
have shown their interest in becoming lawyers will
have an opportunity to prepare and present a defense in student court.

Conclusion RECOMMENDATIONS
To implement this plan, we would need to do the
following:

1. Obtain the approval of your office
2. Obtain the approval of the Provost
3. Establish a procedure by which students can
   obtain legal assistance from peers on campus.

I look forward to discussing this matter with you in
more detail.

35d Writing E-Mails

In many workplaces, virtually all internal (and some external) communications are transmitted as e-mail. Although personal e-mail tends to be quite informal, business e-mail observes the conventions of standard written communication. The following rules can help you communicate effectively in an electronic environment.

✓ CHECKLIST: WRITING E-MAILS

- ✔ Write in complete sentences. Avoid the slang, imprecise diction, and abbreviations that are commonplace in personal e-mail.
- ✔ Use an appropriate tone. Address readers with respect, just as you would in a standard business letter.
- ✔ Include a subject line that clearly identifies your content. If your subject line is vague, your e-mail may be deleted without being read.
- ✔ Make your message as short as possible. Because most e-mails are read on the screen, long discussions are difficult to follow.
- ✔ Use short paragraphs, leaving an extra space between paragraphs.
- ✔ Use lists and internal headings to focus your discussion and to break it into parts. This strategy will make your message easier to understand.
- ✔ Take the time to edit your e-mail after you have written it. Delete excess words and phrases.
- ✔ Proofread carefully before sending your e-mail. Look for errors in grammar, spelling, and punctuation.
- ✔ Make sure that your list of recipients is accurate and that you do not send your e-mail to unintended recipients.
- ✔ Do not send your e-mail until you are absolutely certain that your message says exactly what you want it to say.
- ✔ Do not forward an e-mail unless you have the permission of the sender.
- ✔ Watch what you write. Keep in mind that e-mail written at work is the property of the employer, who has the legal right to access it—even without your permission.

CHAPTER 36

MAKING ORAL PRESENTATIONS

At school and on the job, you may sometimes be called upon to make an oral presentation. In a college course, you might be asked to explain your ideas, to defend your position, or to present your research. At work, you might be asked to discuss a process, propose a project, or solve a problem. Although many people are uncomfortable about making oral presentations, the guidelines that follow can make the process easier and less stressful.

36a Getting Started

Just as with writing an essay, the preparation phase of an oral presentation is as important as the speech itself. The time you spend here will make your job easier later on.

Identify Your Topic The first thing you should do is to identify the topic of your speech. Sometimes you are assigned a topic; at other times you are given the option of choosing your own. Once you have a topic, you should decide how much information, as well as what kind of information, you will need.

Consider Your Audience The easiest way to determine what kind of information you will need is to consider the nature of your audience. Is your audience made up of experts or of people who know very little about your topic? How much background information will you have to provide? Can you use technical terms, or should you avoid them? Do you think your audience will be interested in your topic, or will you have to create interest? What opinions or ideas about your topic will the members of your audience bring with them?

AUDIENCE

An **expert audience** is made up of people who have intimate knowledge of your particular field or subject.

continued on the following page

continued from the previous page

A **collegial audience** is made up of people who share the same frame of reference as you do.

A **general audience** is made up of people who have no specific knowledge of your topic or field.

A **mixed audience** is made up of people who have varying degrees of knowledge about your topic or field.

Consider Your Purpose   Your speech should have a specific purpose that you can sum up concisely—for example, *to argue that the history department should offer a course on the history of copyright law.* To help you zero in on your purpose, ask yourself what you are trying to accomplish with your presentation. Are you trying to inform? To instruct? To stimulate an exchange of ideas? To get support for a project? To solicit feedback? To persuade? It is good a idea to keep this purpose statement in front you on an index card so that it will help keep you focused as you plan your speech.

Consider Your Constraints   How much time do you have for your presentation? (Obviously a ten-minute presentation requires more information and preparation than a three-minute presentation.) Do you already know enough about your topic, or will you have to do research? Where will you go to find information? The library? The Internet? Somewhere else?

36b Planning Your Speech

In the planning phase, you focus your ideas about your topic and develop a thesis; then, you decide what specific points you will discuss and divide your speech into a few manageable sections.

Develop a Thesis Statement   Before you can actually begin to plan your speech, you should develop a thesis statement that clearly and concisely presents your main idea—the key idea you want to present to your audience. For example, the student who wrote the purpose statement above came up with this thesis statement for her speech: *The Department of History needs to develop a course on the history of copyright law.* If you know a lot about your topic, you can develop a thesis on your own. If you do not, you will have to gather information and review it before you can decide on a thesis. As you plan your speech, remember to refer to your thesis to make sure that you stay on track.

Decide on Your Points   Once you have developed a thesis, you can decide what points you will discuss. Unlike readers, who can reread a passage until they understand it, listeners must understand information the first time they hear it. For this reason, speeches usually focus on points that are clear and easy to follow. Frequently, your thesis statement states or strongly implies these points: *There are two broad areas of copyright law that are historically significant and should be taught in a new course offered by the Department of History.*

Outline the Individual Parts of Your Speech   Every speech has a beginning, a middle, and an end. Your **introduction** should introduce your subject, engage your audience's interest, and state your thesis—but it should not present an in-depth discussion or a summary of your topic. The **body,** or middle section, of your speech should present the points that support your thesis. It should also include the facts, examples, and other information that will clarify your points and help convince listeners that your thesis is reasonable. As you present your points, use strong topic sentences to lead listeners from one point to another: *The first step, The second step,* and so on. Your **conclusion** should bring your speech to a definite end and reinforce your thesis. Because an audience remembers best what it hears last, this section is extremely important. In your conclusion, you should restate your thesis and reaffirm how your speech supports it.

36c Preparing Your Notes

Most people use notes of some form when they give a speech. Each system of notes has advantages and disadvantages.

Full Text   Some people like to write out the full text of their speech and refer to it during their presentation. If the type is large enough, and if you triple-space, such notes can be useful. One disadvantage of using of a full text of your speech is that it is easy to lose your place and become disoriented; another is that you may find yourself simply reading your speech. In either case, you not only stop relating to your audience but also lose their interest.

3 × 5 Cards   Some people write parts of their speech—for example, a list of key points or definitions—on 3×5 note-cards, which can be rearranged easily. They are also small, so they can be placed inconspicuously on a podium or a table. With some practice, you can use notecards effectively. You have to be careful, however, not to become so dependent on the cards that you lose eye contact with your audience or begin fidgeting with the cards as you give your speech.

Outlines   Some people like to refer to an outline when they give their speech. As they speak, they can glance down at the outline to get their bearings or to remind themselves of a point they may have forgotten. Because an outline does not contain the full text of a speech, the temptation to read is eliminated. However, if for some reason you draw a blank, an outline gives you very little to fall back on.

Computer Presentation Software   Finally, some people like to use a computer presentation program like Microsoft's *Power-Point* to keep them on track.

As you plan your speech, you should decide whether you want to use some type of visual aid. Visual aids—such as over-

36d   Preparing Visuals

head transparencies, posters, or computer presentation software—can reinforce important information and make your speech easier to understand. They can also break the monotony of a speech and help focus an audience's attention.

For a simple speech, a visual aid may be no more than a definition or a few key terms, names, or dates written on the board. For a more complicated presentation, you might need charts, graphs, diagrams, or photographs—or even objects. The major consideration for including a visual aid is whether it actually adds something to your speech. If a poster will help your listeners understand some key concepts, then by all means use one. However, if it will do little to highlight the information in your speech, then don't use it. Finally, if you are using equipment such as a slide projector or a laptop, make sure you know how to operate it—and have a contingency plan just in case the equipment doesn't work the way it should. For example, it is a good idea to back up a PowerPoint presentation with overhead transparencies just in case the computer at school or at work will not open your files.

If possible, visit the room in which you will be giving your speech, and see whether it has the equipment you need. Some college classrooms are equipped with overhead projectors, VCRs, or computer interfaces. At other schools, you have to make arrangements in advance for equipment.

Finally, make sure that whatever visual aid you use is large enough for everyone in your audience to see. Printing or typing should be neat and free of errors. Graphics should be clearly labeled and easy to see.

✔ CHECKLIST: DESIGNING VISUALS

- ✔ Do not put more than three or four points on a single visual.
- ✔ Use single words or short phrases, not sentences or paragraphs.
- ✔ Limit the number of visuals. For a 3- to 5-minute presentation, five or six visuals are enough.
- ✔ Use the same-size font and the same color consistently on each visual.
- ✔ Use type that is large enough for your audience to see (36-point type for major headings and18-point type for text).
- ✔ Do not use elaborate graphics or special effects just because your computer software enables you to do so (this is especially relevant for users of Microsoft's *PowerPoint*).
- ✔ Check your visuals for correctness. Make sure your graphics do not contain typos, mislabelings, or other kinds of errors.

36e Rehearsing Your Speech

There is a direct relationship between how thoroughly you prepared and how effective your speech is. For this reason, you should practice your speech often—at least five times. Do not try to memorize your entire speech, but be sure you know it well enough so that you can move from point to point without constantly looking at your notes. If possible, rehearse your speech in the actual room you will be using, and try standing in the back of the room to make sure that your visuals can be seen clearly. You should also practice in front of some friends and get some constructive criticism about both the content and the delivery of your speech. Another strategy is to use a tape recorder to help you rehearse. When you play back the tape, you can hear whether you are pronouncing your words clearly and whether you are saying "uh" or "you know" throughout your presentation. Finally, time yourself. Make certain that your 3-minute speech actually takes 3 minutes to deliver.

36f Delivering Your Speech

The most important part of your speech is your delivery. Keep in mind that a certain amount of nervousness is normal, so try not to focus on your nervousness too much. While you are waiting to begin, take some deep breaths and calm down. Once you get to the front of the room, do not start right away. Take the time to make sure that everything you will need is there and that all your equipment is positioned properly.

Before you speak, make sure that both feet are flat on the floor and that you face the audience. When you begin speaking, pace yourself. Speak slowly and clearly, and look at the entire audience, one person at a time. Make sure that you speak *to* your audience, not *at* them. Even though your speech is planned, it should sound natural and conversational. Speak loudly enough for everyone in the room to hear you, and re-member to vary your pitch and your volume so that you do not speak in a monotone. Try using pauses to emphasize important points and to give listeners time to consider what you have said. Finally, sound enthusiastic about your subject. If you appear to be bored or distracted, your audience will be too.

Your movements should be purposeful and natural. Do not pace or lean against something. Move around only when the need arises—for example, to change a visual, to point to a chart, or to distribute something. Never turn your back to your audi-ence; if you have to write on the board, make sure that you are angled toward the audience. Try to use hand movements to em-phasize points, but do not play with pens or notecards as you speak, and do not put your hands in your pockets. Also, resist the temptation to deliver your speech from behind a podium or a table: come around to the front and address the audience directly.

Finally, dress appropriately for the occasion. How you look will be the first thing that listeners notice about you. (Although shorts and a T-shirt may be appropriate for an afternoon in the park, they are not suitable for a classroom presentation.) Dress-ing appropriately not only demonstrates your respect for your audience but also shows that you are someone who deserves to be taken seriously.

PART 9

GRAMMAR, USAGE, AND ESL REVIEW

APPENDIX A

GRAMMAR REVIEW

A1 Parts of Speech

The **part of speech** to which a word belongs depends on its function in a sentence.

(1) Nouns

Nouns name people, animals, places, things, ideas, actions, or qualities.

A **common noun** names any of a class of people, places, or things: *artist, judge, building, event, city.*

A **proper noun,** always **capitalized**, refers to a particular person, place, or thing: *Mary Cassatt, World Trade Center, Crimean War.* See 22a

A **collective noun** designates a group thought of as a unit: *committee, class, family.*

An **abstract noun** refers to an intangible idea or quality: *love, hate, justice, anger, fear, prejudice.*

(2) Pronouns

Pronouns are words used in place of nouns. The noun for which a pronoun stands is its **antecedent.**

Although different types of pronouns may have the same form, they are distinguished from one another by their function in a sentence.

A **personal pronoun** stands for a person or thing: *I, me, we, us, my, mine, our, ours, you, your, yours, he, she, it, its, him, his, her, hers, they, them, their, theirs.*

They made her an offer she couldn't refuse.

An **indefinite pronoun** does not refer to any particular person or thing, so it does not require an antecedent. Indefinite pronouns include *another, any, each, few, many, some, nothing, one, anyone, everyone, everybody, everything, someone, something, either,* and *neither.* See 5a4, 5b3

Many are called, but few are chosen.

A **reflexive pronoun** ends with *-self* and refers to a recipient of the action that is the same as the actor: *myself, yourself, himself, herself, itself, oneself, themselves, ourselves, yourselves.*

They found themselves in downtown Pittsburgh.

259

Intensive pronouns have the same form as reflexive pronouns; an intensive pronoun emphasizes a preceding noun or pronoun.

Darrow <u>himself</u> was sure his client was innocent.

A **relative pronoun** introduces an adjective or noun clause in a sentence. Relative pronouns include *which, who, whom, that, what, whose, whatever, whoever, whomever,* and *whichever.*

Gandhi was the man <u>who</u> led India to independence. (introduces adjective clause)

<u>Whatever</u> happens will be a surprise. (introduces noun clause)

An **interrogative pronoun** introduces a question. Interrogative pronouns include *who, which, what, whom, whose, whoever, whatever,* and *whichever.*

<u>Who</u> was that masked man?

A **demonstrative pronoun** points to a particular thing or group of things. *This, that, these,* and *those* are demonstrative pronouns.

<u>This</u> is one of Shakespeare's early plays.

A **reciprocal pronoun** denotes a mutual relationship. The reciprocal pronouns are *each other* and *one another. Each other* indicates a relationship between two individuals; *one another* denotes a relationship among more than two.

Cathy and I respect <u>each other</u> for our differences.

Many of our friends do not respect <u>one another</u>.

(3) Verbs

Verbs can be classified into two groups: *main verbs* and *auxiliary verbs.*

Main Verbs **Main verbs** carry most of the meaning in a sentence or clause. Some main verbs are action verbs.

He <u>ran</u> for the train. (physical action)

He <u>thought</u> about taking the bus. (emotional action)

Other main verbs are linking verbs. A **linking verb** does not show any physical or emotional action. Its function is to link the subject to a **subject complement,** a word or phrase that renames or describes the subject. Linking verbs include *be, become,* and *seem* and verbs that describe sensations—*look, appear, feel, taste, smell,* and so on.

Carbon disulfide <u>smells</u> bad.

Auxiliary Verbs **Auxiliary verbs** (also called **helping verbs**), such as *be* and *have,* combine with main verbs to form **verb phrases.** Auxiliary verbs indicate tense, voice, or mood.

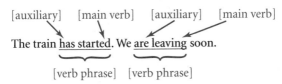

[auxiliary]   [main verb]   [auxiliary]   [main verb]

The train <u>has started</u>. We <u>are leaving</u> soon.

[verb phrase]   [verb phrase]

Certain auxiliary verbs, known as **modal auxiliaries,** indicate necessity, possibility, willingness, obligation, or ability. These include *must, shall, might, will, should, can, would, may, could, need* [to], and *ought* [to].

Verbals **Verbals,** such as *known* or *running* or *to go,* are verb forms that act as adjectives, adverbs, or nouns. A verbal can never serve as a sentence's main verb unless it is used with one or more auxiliary verbs (He *is* running). Verbals include *participles, infinitives,* and *gerunds.*

Participles Virtually every verb has a **present participle,** which ends in *-ing* (*loving, learning*) and a **past participle,** which usually ends in *-d* or *-ed* (*agreed, learned*). Some verbs have <u>**irregular**</u> past participles (*gone, begun, written*). Participles may function in a sentence as adjectives or as nouns.

See 6a

Twenty brands of <u>running</u> shoes were on display. (participle serves as adjective)

The <u>wounded</u> were given emergency first aid. (participle serves as noun)

Infinitives An **infinitive**—the *to* form of the verb—may function as an adjective, an adverb, or a noun.

Ann Arbor was clearly the place <u>to be</u>. (infinitive serves as adjective)

Carla went outside <u>to think</u>. (infinitive serves as adverb)

<u>To win</u> was everything. (infinitive serves as subject)

Gerunds **Gerunds,** which like present participles end in *-ing,* always function as nouns.

<u>Seeing</u> is <u>believing</u>.

Andrew loves <u>skiing</u>.

(4) Adjectives

Adjectives describe, limit, qualify, or in some other way modify nouns or pronouns.

Descriptive adjectives name a quality of the noun or pronoun they modify.

After the game, they were <u>exhausted</u>.

They ordered a <u>chocolate</u> soda and a <u>butterscotch</u> sundae.

When articles, pronouns, numbers, and the like function as adjectives, limiting or qualifying nouns or pronouns, they are referred to as **determiners**.

See C1.3

(5) Adverbs

Adverbs describe the action of verbs or modify adjectives or other adverbs (or complete phrases, clauses, or sentences). They answer the questions "How?" "Why?" "When?" "Under what conditions?" and "To what extent?"

He walked <u>rather hesitantly</u> toward the front of the room.

Let's meet <u>tomorrow</u> for coffee.

Adverbs that modify other adverbs or adjectives limit or qualify the words they modify.

He pitched an <u>almost perfect</u> game yesterday.

Interrogative Adverbs The **interrogative adverbs** (*how, when, why,* and *where*) introduce questions.

See 2b

Conjuctive Adverbs **Conjunctive adverbs** act as **transitional words**, joining and relating independent clauses.

FREQUENTLY USED CONJUNCTIVE ADVERBS

accordingly	furthermore	meanwhile	similarly
also	hence	moreover	still
anyway	however	nevertheless	then
besides	incidentally	next	thereafter
certainly	indeed	nonetheless	therefore
consequently	instead	now	thus
finally	likewise	otherwise	undoubtedly

---

(6) Prepositions

A **preposition** introduces a noun or pronoun (or a phrase or clause functioning in the sentence as a noun), linking it to other words in the sentence. The word or word group that the preposition introduces is its **object**.

$$\text{prep} \quad \text{obj} \qquad \text{prep} \quad \text{obj}$$

They received a postcard <u>from</u> Bobby telling <u>about</u> his trip.

FREQUENTLY USED PREPOSITIONS

about	beneath	inside	since
above	beside	into	through
across	between	like	throughout
after	beyond	near	to
against	by	of	toward
along	concerning	off	under
among	despite	on	underneath
around	down	onto	until
as	during	out	up
at	except	outside	upon
before	for	over	with
behind	from	past	within
below	in	regarding	without

---

(7) Conjunctions

Conjunctions connect words, phrases, clauses, or sentences.

Coordinating Conjunctions **Coordinating conjunctions** (*and, or, but, nor, for, so, yet*) connect words, phrases, or clauses of equal weight.

Should I order chicken <u>or</u> fish?

Thoreau wrote *Walden* in 1854, <u>and</u> he died in 1862.

Correlative Conjunctions Always used in pairs, **correlative conjunctions** also link items of equal weight.

<u>Both</u> Hancock <u>and</u> Jefferson signed the Declaration of Independence.

<u>Either</u> I will renew my lease, <u>or</u> I will move.

FREQUENTLY USED CORRELATIVE CONJUNCTIONS

both . . . and	neither . . . nor
either . . . or	not only . . . but also
just as . . . so	whether . . . or

Subordinating Conjunctions Words such as *since, because,* and *although* are **subordinating conjunctions.** They introduce adverb clauses and thus connect the sentence's independent (main) clause to a dependent (subordinate) clause to form a **complex sentence**.

See 9a2

<u>Although</u> people may feel healthy, they can still have medical problems.

It is best to diagram your garden <u>before</u> you start to plant.

(8) Interjections

Interjections **Interjections** are words used as exclamations to express emotion: *Oh! Ouch! Wow! Alas! Hey!*

A2 Sentences

(1) Basic Sentence Elements

A **sentence** is an independent grammatical unit that contains a <u>subject</u> and a <u>predicate</u> and expresses a complete thought.

The quick brown fox <u>jumped over the lazy dog</u>.

It <u>came from outer space</u>.

(2) Basic Sentence Patterns

A **simple sentence** consists of at least one subject and one predicate. Simple sentences conform to one of five patterns.

Subject + Intransitive Verb (s + v)

$$\underset{\text{s}}{\text{Stock prices}} \ \underset{\text{v}}{\underline{\text{may fall}}}.$$

Subject + Transitive Verb + Direct Object (s + v + do)

Van Gogh <u>created</u> *The Starry Night*.
  s   v   do

Caroline <u>saved</u> Jake.
  s   v   do

Subject + Transitive Verb + Direct Object + Object Complement (s + v + do + oc)

I <u>found</u> the exam easy.
s   v   do   oc

The class <u>elected</u> Bridget treasurer.
  s   v   do   oc

Subject + Linking Verb + Subject Complement (s + v + sc)

The injection <u>was</u> painless.
    s   v   sc

Tony Blair <u>became</u> prime minister.
   s   v   sc

Subject + Transitive Verb + Indirect Object + Direct Object
(s + v + io + do)

    s   v   io   do
<u>Cyrano</u> <u>wrote</u> Roxanne a poem. (Cyrano wrote a poem *for* Roxanne.)

    s   v   io   do
<u>Hester</u> <u>gave</u> Pearl a kiss. (Hester gave a kiss *to* Pearl.)

(3) Phrases and Clauses

A **phrase** is a group of related words that lacks a subject or predicate or both and functions as a single part of speech. It cannot stand alone as a sentence.

A **verb phrase** consists of a **main verb** and all its auxiliary verbs. (Time *is flying*.) A **noun phrase** includes a noun or pronoun plus all related modifiers. (I'll climb *the highest mountain*.) See A1.6

A **prepositional phrase** consists of a <u>preposition</u>, its object, and any modifiers of that object (They considered the ethical implications *of the animal studies*).

A **verbal phrase** consists of a <u>verbal</u> and its related objects, modifiers, or complements. A verbal phrase may be a **participial phrase** (*encouraged by the voter turnout*), a **gerund phrase** (*taking it easy*), or an **infinitive phrase** (*to evaluate the evidence*). See A1.3

An **absolute phrase** usually consists of a noun and a participle, accompanied by modifiers. It modifies an entire independent clause rather than a particular word or phrase.

<u>Their toes tapping</u>, they watched the auditions.

A **clause** is a group of related words that includes a subject and a predicate. An **independent** (main) **clause** may stand alone as a sentence, but a **dependent** (subordinate) **clause** cannot. It must always be combined with an independent clause to form a <u>complex sentence.</u> See 9a2

[Lucretia Mott was an abolitionist.] [She was also a pioneer for women's rights.] (two independent clauses)

[Lucretia Mott was an abolitionist] [who was also a pioneer for women's rights.] (independent clause, dependent clause)

Dependent clauses may be adjective, adverb, or noun clauses.

Adjective clauses, sometimes called **relative clauses,** modify nouns or pronouns and always follow the nouns or pronouns they modify. They are introduced by relative pronouns—*that, what, which, who,* and so forth—or by the adverbs *where* and *when.*

Celeste's grandparents, <u>who were born in Romania</u>, speak little English.

Adverb clauses modify verbs, adjectives, adverbs, entire phrases, or independent clauses. They are always introduced by subordinating conjunctions.

Mark will go <u>wherever there's a party</u>.

Noun clauses function as subjects, objects, or complements. A noun clause may be introduced by a relative pronoun or by *whether, when, where, why,* or *how.*

<u>What you see</u> is <u>what you get</u>.

(4) Types of Sentences

A **simple sentence** is a single independent clause. A simple sentence can consist of just a subject and a predicate.

<u>Jessica</u> <u>fell</u>.

Or, a simple sentence can be expanded with modifying words and phrases.

Jessica fell in love with the mysterious Henry Goodyear on Halloween.

See
9a1   A <u>**compound sentence**</u> consists of two or more simple sentences linked by a coordinating conjunction (preceded by a comma), by a semicolon (alone or with a transitional word or phrase), by correlative conjunctions, or by a colon.

[The moon rose in the sky], <u>and</u> [the stars shone brightly].

[José wanted to spend a quiet afternoon]; <u>however,</u> [his aunt surprised him with a new set of plans.]

See
9a2   A <u>**complex sentence**</u> consists of an independent clause along with one or more dependent clauses.

     Independent clause   Dependent clause
[It was hard for us to believe] [that anyone could be so cruel].

A **compound-complex sentence** is a compound sentence—made up of at least two independent clauses—that also includes at least one dependent clause.

[My mother always worried] [when my father had to work late], and [she could rarely sleep more than a few minutes at a time].

Sentences can also be classified according to their function. **Declarative sentences** make statements; they are the most common. **Interrogative sentences** pose questions, usually by inverting standard subject-verb order (often with an interrogative word) or by adding a form of *do* (*Is Maggie at home? Where is Maggie? Does Maggie live here?*). **Imperative sentences** express commands or requests, using the second-person singular of the verb and generally omitting the pronoun subject *you* (*Go to your room. Please believe me.*). **Exclamatory sentences** express strong emotion and end with an exclamation point (*The killing must stop now!*).

APPENDIX B

USAGE REVIEW

This usage review lists words and phrases that are often troublesome for writers.

a, an   Use *a* before words that begin with consonants and words that have initial vowels that sound like consonants: *a* person, *a* one-horse carriage, *a* uniform. Use *an* before words that begin with vowels and words that begin with a silent *h: an* artist, *an* honest person.

accept, except   *Accept* is a verb that means "to receive"; *except* as a preposition or conjunction means "other than" and as a verb means "to leave out": The auditors will *accept* all your claims *except* the last two. Some businesses are *excepted* from the regulation.

advice, advise   *Advice* is a noun meaning "opinion or information offered"; *advise* is a verb that means "to offer advice to": The broker *advised* her client to take his attorney's *advice.*

affect, effect   *Affect* is a verb meaning "to influence"; *effect* can be a verb or a noun. As a verb it means "to bring about," and as a noun it means "result": We know how the drug *affects* patients immediately, but little is known of its long-term *effects*. The arbitrator tried to *effect* a settlement between the parties.

all ready, already   *All ready* means "completely prepared"; *Already* means "by or before this or that time": I was *all ready* to help, but it was *already* too late.

all right, alright   Although the use of *alright* is increasing, current usage calls for *all right.*

allusion, illusion   An *allusion* is a reference or hint; an *illusion* is something that is not what it seems: The poem makes an *allusion* to the Pandora myth. The shadows created an optical *illusion*.

a lot   *A lot* is always two words.

among, between   *Among* refers to groups of more than two things; *between* refers to just two things: The three parties agreed *among* themselves to settle the case. There will be a brief intermission *between* the two acts.

amount, number   *Amount* refers to a quantity that cannot be counted; *number* refers to things that can be counted: Even a small *amount* of caffeine can be harmful. Seeing their commander fall, a large *number* of troops ran to his aid.

an, a   See **a, an.**

and/or   In business or technical writing, use *and/or* when either or both of the items it connects can apply. In college writing, however, the use of *and/or* should generally be avoided.

as . . . as . . .   In such constructions, *as* signals a comparison; therefore, you must always use the second *as*: *East of Eden* is *as* long *as The Grapes of Wrath*.

as, like   *As* can be used as a conjunction (to introduce a complete clause) or as a preposition; *like* should be used as a preposition only: In *The Scarlet Letter* Hawthorne uses imagery *as* (not *like*) he does in his other works. After classes he works *as* a manager of a fast-food restaurant. Writers *like* Carl Sandburg appear once in a generation.

at, to   Many people use the prepositions *at* and *to* after *where* in conversation: *Where* are you working *at*? *Where* are you going *to*? This usage is redundant and should not appear in college writing.

awhile, a while   *Awhile* is an adverb; *a while*, which consists of an article and a noun, is used as the object of a preposition: Before we continue we will rest *awhile*. (modifies the verb *rest*); Before we continue we will rest for *a while*. (object of the preposition *for*)

bad, badly   *Bad* is an adjective, and *badly* is an adverb: The school board decided that *Huckleberry Finn* was a *bad* book. American automobile makers did not do *badly* this year. After verbs that refer to any of the senses or after any other linking verb, use the adjective form: He looked *bad*. He felt *bad*. It seemed *bad*.

being as, being that   These awkward phrases add unnecessary words and weaken your writing. Use *because* instead.

beside, besides   *Beside* is a preposition meaning "next to"; *besides* can be either a preposition meaning "except" or "other than," or an adverb meaning "as well": *Beside* the tower was a wall that ran the length of the city. *Besides* its industrial uses, laser technology has many other applications. Edison invented not only the lightbulb but the phonograph *besides*.

between, among   See **among, between.**

bring, take   *Bring* means to transport from a farther place to a nearer place; *take* means to carry or convey from a nearer place to a farther one: *Bring* me a souvenir from your trip. *Take* this message to the general, and wait for a reply.

can, may   *Can* denotes ability, and *may* indicates permission: If you *can* play, you *may* use my piano.

capital, capitol   *Capital* refers to a city that is an official seat of government; *capitol* refers to a building in which a legislature meets: Washington, DC, is the *capital* of the United States. When we were there, we visited the *Capitol* building.

center around   This imprecise phrase is acceptable in speech and informal writing but not in college writing. Use *center on* instead.

cite, site   Cite is a verb meaning "to quote as an authority or example"; *site* is a noun meaning "a place or setting": Jeff *cited* five sources in his research paper. The builder cleared the *site* for the new bank.

climactic, climatic   Climactic means "of or related to a climax"; *climatic* means "of or related to climate": The *climactic* moment of the movie occurs unexpectedly. If scientists are correct, the *climatic* conditions of Earth are changing.

coarse, course   Coarse is an adjective meaning "inferior" or "having a rough, uneven texture"; *course* is a noun meaning "a route or path," "an area on which a sport is played," or "a unit of study": *Coarse* sandpaper is used to smooth the surface. The *course* of true love never runs smoothly. Last semester I had to drop a *course*.

complement, compliment   Complement means "to complete or add to"; *compliment* means "to give praise": A double-blind study would *complement* their preliminary research. My instructor *complimented* me on my improvement.

conscious, conscience   Conscious is an adjective meaning "having one's mental faculties awake"; *conscience* is a noun that means the moral sense of right and wrong: The patient will remain *conscious* during the procedure. His *conscience* wouldn't allow him to lie.

continual, continuous   Continual means "recurring at intervals"; *continuous* refers to an action that occurs without interruption: A pulsar is a star that emits a *continual* stream of electromagnetic radiation. (It emits radiation at regular intervals.) A small battery allows the watch to run *continuously* for five years. (It runs without stopping.)

could of, should of, would of   The contractions *could've, should've,* and *would've* are often misspelled as the nonstandard constructions *could of, should of,* and *would of.* Use *could have, should have,* and *would have* in college writing.

council, counsel   A council is "a body of people who serve in a legislative or advisory capacity"; *counsel* means "to offer advice or guidance": The city *council* argued about the proposed ban on smoking. The judge *counseled* the couple to settle their differences.

couple of   Couple means "a pair," but *couple of* is used colloquially to mean "several" or "a few." In your college writing, specify "four points" or "two examples" rather than using "a couple of."

criterion, criteria   Criteria, from the Greek, is the plural of *criterion,* meaning "standard for judgment": Of all the *criteria* for hiring graduating seniors, class rank is the most important *criterion.*

data   Data is the plural of the Latin *datum,* meaning "fact." In everyday speech and writing, *data* is used for both singular and plural. In college writing, you should use *data* only for the plural: The *data* discussed in this section *are* summarized in Appendix A.

different from, different than   *Different than* is widely used in American speech. In college writing, use *different from*.

discreet, discrete   *Discreet* means "careful or prudent"; *discrete* means "separate or individually distinct": Because Madame Bovary was not *discreet,* her reputation suffered. Atoms can be broken into hundreds of *discrete* particles.

disinterested, uninterested   *Disinterested* means "objective" or "capable of making an impartial judgment"; *uninterested* means "indifferent or unconcerned": The American judicial system depends on *disinterested* jurors. Finding no treasure, Hernando de Soto was *uninterested* in going farther.

don't, doesn't   *Don't* is the contraction of *do not; doesn't* is the contraction of *does not.* Do not confuse the two: My dog *doesn't* (not *don't*) like to walk in the rain.

effect, affect   See **affect, effect.**

e.g.   *E.g.* is an abbreviation for the Latin *exempli gratia,* meaning "for example" or "for instance." Use *e.g.* only in parenthetical material.

emigrate from, immigrate to   To *emigrate* is "to leave one's country and settle in another"; to *immigrate* is "to come to another country and reside there." The noun forms of these words are *emigrant* and *immigrant*: My great-grandfather *emigrated from* Warsaw along with many other *emigrants* from Poland. Many people *immigrate* to the United States for economic reasons, but such *immigrants* still face great challenges.

eminent, imminent   *Eminent* is an adjective meaning "standing above others" or "prominent"; *imminent* means "about to occur": Oliver Wendell Holmes, Jr., was an *eminent* jurist. In ancient times, a comet signaled *imminent* disaster.

enthused   *Enthused,* a colloquial form of *enthusiastic,* should not be used in college writing.

etc.   *Etc.,* the abbreviation of *et cetera,* means "and the rest." Use *etc.* only with parenthetical material. Otherwise, say "and so on" or, better, specify exactly what *etc.* stands for.

everyday, every day   *Everyday* is an adjective that means "ordinary" or "commonplace"; *every day* means "occurring daily": In the Gettysburg Address, Lincoln used *everyday* language. She exercises almost *every day*.

everyone, every one   *Everyone* is an indefinite pronoun meaning "every person"; *every one* means "every individual or thing in a particular group": *Everyone* seems happier in the spring. *Every one* of the packages had been opened.

except, accept   See **accept, except.**

explicit, implicit   *Explicit* means "expressed or stated directly"; *implicit* means "implied" or "expressed or stated indirectly": The director *explicitly* warned the actors to be on time for rehearsals. Her *implicit* message was that lateness would not be tolerated.

farther, further   *Farther* designates distance; *further* designates degree: I have traveled *farther* from home than any of my relatives. Critics charge that welfare subsidies encourage *further* dependence.

fewer, less   Use *fewer* with nouns that can be counted: *fewer* books, *fewer* people, *fewer* dollars. Use *less* with quantities that cannot be counted: *less* pain, *less* power, *less* enthusiasm.

firstly (secondly, thirdly, . . .)   Archaic forms meaning "in the first . . . second . . . third place." Use *first, second, third.*

further, farther   See **farther, further.**

good, well   *Good* is an adjective, never an adverb: She is a *good* swimmer. *Well* can function as an adverb or as an adjective. As an adverb it means "in a good manner": She swam *well* (not *good*) in the meet. *Well* is used as an adjective with verbs that denote a state of being or feeling. Here *well* can mean "in good health": I feel *well.*

got to   *Got to* is not acceptable in college writing. To indicate obligation, use *have to, has to,* or *must.*

hanged, hung   Both *hanged* and *hung* are past participles of *hang. Hanged* is used to refer to executions; *hung* is used to mean "suspended": Billy Budd was *hanged* for killing the master-at-arms. The stockings were *hung* by the chimney with care.

he, she   Traditionally *he* has been used in the generic sense to refer to both males and females. To acknowledge the equality of the sexes, however, avoid the generic *he.* Use plural pronouns whenever possible. See **14d.2.**

hopefully   The adverb *hopefully,* meaning "in a hopeful manner," should modify a verb, an adjective, or another adverb. Do not use *hopefully* as a sentence modifier meaning "it is hoped." Rather than "*Hopefully,* scientists will soon discover a cure for AIDS," write "Scientists *hope* they will soon discover a cure for AIDS."

i.e.   *I.e.* is an abbreviation for the Latin *id est,* meaning "that is." Use *i.e.* only with parenthetical material.

if, whether   When asking indirect questions or expressing doubt, use *whether:* He asked *whether* (not *if*) the flight would be delayed. The flight attendant was not sure *whether* (not *if*) it would be delayed.

illusion, allusion   See **allusion, illusion.**

immigrate to, emigrate from   See **emigrate from, immigrate to.**

implicit, explicit   See **explicit, implicit.**

imply, infer   *Imply* means "to hint" or "to suggest"; *infer* means "to conclude from": Mark Antony *implied* that the conspirators had murdered Caesar. The crowd *inferred* his meaning and called for justice.

infer, imply   See **imply, infer.**

inside of, outside of   *Of* is unnecessary when *inside* and *outside* are used as prepositions. *Inside of* is colloquial in references to time: He waited *inside* (not *inside of*) the coffee shop. He could run a mile in *under* (not *inside of*) eight minutes.

irregardless, regardless   *Irregardless* is a nonstandard version of *regardless*. Use *regardless* instead.

is when, is where   These constructions are faulty when they appear in definitions: A playoff *is* an additional game played to establish the winner of a tie. (not "A playoff *is when* an additional game is played. . . . ")

its, it's   *Its* is a possessive pronoun; *it's* is a contraction of *it is*: It's no secret that the bank is out to protect *its* assets.

kind of, sort of   *Kind of* and *sort of* to mean "rather" or "somewhat" are colloquial and should not appear in college writing: It is well known that Napoleon was *rather* (not *kind of*) short.

lay, lie   See **lie, lay.**

leave, let   *Leave* means "to go away from" or "to let remain"; *let* means "to allow" or "to permit": *Let* (not *leave*) me give you a hand.

less, fewer   See **fewer, less.**

let, leave   See **leave, let.**

lie, lay   *Lie* is an intransitive verb (one that does not take an object) that means "to recline." Its principal forms are *lie, lay, lain, lying*: Each afternoon she would *lie* in the sun and listen to the surf. *As I Lay Dying* is a novel by William Faulkner. By 1871, Troy had *lain* undisturbed for two thousand years. The painting shows a nude *lying* on a couch. *Lay* is a transitive verb (one that takes an object) meaning "to put" or "to place." Its principal forms are *lay, laid, laid, laying*: The Federalist Papers *lay* the foundation for American conservatism. In October of 1781, the British *laid* down their arms and surrendered. He had *laid* his money on the counter before leaving. We watched the stonemasons *laying* a wall.

like, as   See **as, like.**

loose, lose   *Loose* is an adjective meaning "not rigidly fastened or securely attached"; *lose* is a verb meaning "to misplace": The marble facing of the building became *loose* and fell to the sidewalk. After only two drinks, most people *lose* their ability to judge distance.

lots, lots of, a lot of   These words are colloquial substitutes for *many, much,* or *a great deal of.* Avoid their use in college writing: The students had many (not *lots of* or *a lot of*) options for essay topics.

man   Like the generic pronoun *he, man* has been used in English to denote members of both sexes. This usage is being replaced by *human beings, people,* or similar terms that do not specify gender. See **14d.2.**

may, can   See **can, may.**

may be, maybe   *May be* is a verb phrase; *maybe* is an adverb meaning "perhaps": She *may be* the smartest student in the class. *Maybe* her experience has given her an advantage.

media, medium   *Medium,* meaning a "means of conveying or broadcasting something," is singular; *media* is the plural form and requires a plural verb: The *media* have distorted the issue.

might have, might of   *Might of* is a nonstandard spelling of the contraction of *might have* (*might've*).

number, amount   See **amount, number.**

OK, O.K., okay   All three spellings are acceptable, but this term should be avoided in college writing. Replace it with a more specific word or words: The lecture was *adequate* (not *okay*), if uninspiring.

outside of, inside of   See **inside of, outside of.**

passed, past   *Passed* is the past tense of the verb *pass; past* means "belonging to a former time" or "no longer current": The car must have been going eighty miles per hour when it *passed* us. In the envelope was a bill marked *past* due.

percent, percentage   *Percent* indicates a part of a hundred when a specific number is referred to: "*ten percent* of his salary." *Percentage* is used when no specific number is referred to: "a *percentage* of next year's receipts." In technical and business writing, it is permissible to use the number and the % sign after percentages you are comparing. write out *percent* in college writing.

phenomenon, phenomena   A *phenomenon* is a single observable fact or event. It can also refer to a rare or significant occurrence. *Phenomena* is the plural form and requires a plural verb: Many supposedly paranormal *phenomena* are easily explained.

plus   As a preposition, *plus* means "in addition to." Avoid using *plus* as a substitute for *moreover* or *and:* Include the principal, *plus* the interest, in your calculations. Your quote was too high; moreover (not *plus*), it was inaccurate.

precede, proceed   *Precede* means "to go or come before"; *proceed* means "to go forward in an orderly way": Robert Frost's *North of Boston* was *preceded* by an earlier volume. In 1532, Francisco Pizarro landed at Tumbes and *proceeded* south.

principal, principle   As a noun, *principal* means "a sum of money (minus interest) invested or lent" or "a person in the leading position"; as an adjective it means "most important." A *principle* is a rule of conduct or a basic truth: He wanted to reduce the *principal* of the loan. The *principal* of the high school is a talented administrator. Women are the *principal* wage earners in many American households. The Constitution embodies certain fundamental *principles.*

quote, quotation   *Quote* is a verb. *Quotation* is a noun. In college writing, do not use *quote* as a shortened form of *quotation:* Scholars attribute those *quotations* (not *quotes*) to Shakespeare.

raise, rise   *Raise* is a transitive verb, and *rise* is an intransitive verb—that is, *raise* takes an object, and *rise* does not: My grandparents *raised* a large family. The sun will *rise* at 6:12 this morning.

real, really   *Real* means "genuine" or "authentic"; *really* means "actually." In your college writing, do not use *real* as an adjective meaning "very."

reason is that, reason is because   *Reason* should be used with *that* and not with *because*, which is redundant: The *reason* he left *is that* (not *is because*) you insulted him.

regardless, irregardless   See **irregardless, regardless.**

respectably, respectfully, respectively   *Respectably* means "worthy of respect"; *respectfully* means "giving honor or deference"; *respectively* means "in the order given": He skated quite *respectably* at his first Olympics. The seminar taught us to treat others *respectfully*. The first- and second-place winners were Tai and Kim, *respectively*.

rise, raise   See **raise, rise.**

set, sit   *Set* means "to put down" or "to lay." Its principal forms are *set* and *setting*: After rocking the baby to sleep, he *set* her down carefully in her crib. *Sit* means "to assume a sitting position." Its principal forms are *sit, sat, sat,* and *sitting*: Many children *sit* in front of the television five to six hours a day.

shall, will   *Will* has all but replaced *shall* to express all future action.

should of   See **could of, should of, would of.**

since   Do not use *since* for *because* if there is any chance of confusion. In the sentence "*Since* President Nixon traveled to China, trade between China and the United States has increased," *since* could mean either "from the time that" or "because."

sit, set   See **set, sit.**

so   Avoid using *so* alone as a vague intensifier meaning "very" or "extremely." Follow *so* with *that* and a clause that describes the result: She was *so* pleased with their work *that* she took them out to lunch.

sometime, sometimes, some time   *Sometime* means "at some time in the future"; *sometimes* means "now and then"; *some time* means "a period of time": The president will address Congress *sometime* next week. All automobiles, no matter how reliable, *sometimes* need repairs. It has been *some time* since I read that book.

sort of, kind of   See **kind of, sort of.**

stationary, stationery   *Stationary* means "staying in one place"; *stationery* means "materials for writing" or "letter paper": The communications satellite appears to be *stationary* in the sky. The secretaries supply departmental offices with *stationery*.

supposed to, used to   *Supposed to* and *used to* are often misspelled. Both verbs require the final *d* to indicate past tense.

take, bring   See **bring, take.**

than, then   *Than* is a conjunction used to indicate a comparison; *then* is an adverb indicating time: The new shopping center is bigger *than* the old one. He did his research; *then* he wrote a report.

that, which, who   Use *that* or *which* when referring to a thing; use *who* when referring to a person: It was a speech *that* inspired many. The movie, *which* was a huge success, failed to impress her. Anyone *who* (not *that*) takes the course will benefit.

their, there, they're   *Their* is a possessive pronoun; *there* indicates place and is also used in the expressions *there is* and *there are*; *they're* is a contraction of *they are*: Watson and Crick did *their* DNA work at Cambridge University. I love Los Angeles, but I wouldn't want to live *there*. *There* is nothing we can do to resurrect an extinct species. When *they're* well treated, rabbits make excellent pets.

themselves; theirselves, theirself   *Theirselves* and *theirself* are nonstandard variants of *themselves*.

then, than   See **than, then.**

till, until, 'til   *Till* and *until* have the same meaning, and both are acceptable. *Until* is preferred in college writing. *'Til,* a contraction of *until,* should be avoided.

to, at   See **at, to.**

to, too, two   *To* is a preposition that indicates direction; *too* is an adverb that means "also" or "more than is needed"; *two* expresses the number 2: Last year we flew from New York *to* California. "Tippecanoe and Tyler, *too*" was Harrison's campaign slogan. The plot was *too* complicated for the average reader. Just north of *Two* Rivers, Wisconsin, is a petrified forest.

try to, try and   *Try and* is the colloquial equivalent of *try to*: He decided to *try to* (not *try and*) do better.

-type   Deleting this empty suffix eliminates clutter and clarifies meaning: Found in the wreckage was an *incendiary* (not *incendiary-type*) device.

uninterested, disinterested   See **disinterested, uninterested.**

unique   Because *unique* means "the only one," not "remarkable" or "unusual," you should never use constructions like "the most unique" or "very unique."

until   See **till, until, 'til.**

used to   See **supposed to, used to.**

utilize   In most cases, it is best to replace *utilize* with *use* (*utilize* often sounds pretentious).

wait for, wait on   To *wait for* means "to defer action until something occurs." To *wait on* means "to act as a waiter": I am *waiting for* (not *on*) dinner.

weather, whether   Weather is a noun meaning "the state of the atmosphere"; *whether* is a conjunction used to introduce an alternative: The *weather* outside is frightful, but the fire inside is delightful. It is doubtful *whether* we will be able to ski tomorrow.

well, good   See **good, well.**

were, we're   Were is a verb; *we're* is the contraction of *we are:* The Trojans *were* asleep when the Greeks attacked. We must act now if *we're* going to succeed.

whether, if   See **if, whether.**

which, who, that   See **that, which, who.**

who, whom   When a pronoun serves as the subject of its clause, use *who* or *whoever;* when it functions in a clause as an object, use *whom* or *whomever:* Sarah, *who* is studying ancient civilizations, would like to visit Greece. Sarah, *whom* I met in France, wants me to travel to Greece with her. To determine which to use at the beginning of a question, use a personal pronoun to answer the question: *Who* tried to call me? *He* called. (subject); *Whom* do you want for the job? I want *her.* (object)

who's, whose   Who's means "who is"; *whose* indicates possession: Who's going to take calculus? The writer *whose* book was in the window was autographing copies.

will, shall   See **shall, will.**

would of   See **could of, should of, would of.**

your, you're   Your indicates possession, and *you're* is the contraction of *you are:* You can improve *your* stamina by jogging two miles a day. *You're* certain to be the winner.

APPENDIX C

ESL REVIEW

✔ CHECKLIST: ENGLISH LANGUAGE BASICS

✔ **In English, words may change their form according to their function.** For example, verbs change form to communicate whether an action is taking place in the past, present, or future.

✔ **In English, context is extremely important to understanding function.** In the following sentences, for instance, the very same words can perform different functions according to their relationships to other words.

Juan and I are taking a <u>walk</u>. (*Walk* is a noun, a direct object of the verb *taking,* with an article, *a,* attached to it.)

If you <u>walk</u> instead of driving, you will help conserve the Earth's resources. (*Walk* is a verb, the predicate of the subject *you.*)

See
Ch. 21

✔ **Spelling in English is not always phonetic and sometimes may seem illogical.** <u>Spelling</u> in English may be related more to the history of the word and to its origins in other languages than to the way the word is pronounced. Therefore, learning to spell correctly is often a matter of memorization, not sounding out the word phonetically. For example, "ough" is pronounced differently in *tough, though,* and *thought.*

See
C6

✔ <u>**Word order**</u> **is extremely important in English sentences.** In English sentences, word order may indicate which word is the subject of the sentence and which is the object, whether the sentence is a question or a statement, and so on.

C1 Nouns

A **noun** names things: people, animals, objects, places, feelings, ideas. If a noun names one thing, it is **singular**; if a noun names many things, it is **plural**.

See
21b7

(1) Noncount Nouns

Some English nouns do not have a plural form. These are called **noncount nouns** because what they name cannot be counted.

NONCOUNT NOUNS

The following commonly used nouns are noncount nouns. These words have no plural forms. Therefore, you should never add *s* to them.

advice	homework
clothing	information
education	knowledge
equipment	luggage
evidence	merchandise
furniture	revenge

(2) Articles with Nouns

English has two **articles:** *a* and *the. A* is called the **indefinite** article; *the* is the **definite article.** *A* is replaced by *an* if the word that follows begins with a *vowel* (*a, e, i, o,* or *u*) or with a vowel *sound: a* book, *an* apple, *an* honor. If the vowel is pronounced like a consonant, use *a: a one-time offer.*

Use an **indefinite article** (*a* or *an*) with a noun when the reader has no reason to be familiar with the noun you are naming—when you are introducing the noun for the first time, for example. To say, "Jatin entered *a* building," signals to the audience that you are introducing the idea of the building for the first time. The building is indefinite, or not specific, until it has been identified.

Use the **definite article** (*the*) when the noun you are naming has already been introduced. To say, "Jatin walked through *the* building," signals to readers that you are referring to the same building you mentioned earlier.

USING ARTICLES WITH NOUNS

There are two exceptions to the rules governing the use of articles with nouns.

- **Plural nouns** do not require **indefinite articles:** "I love horses," not "I love <u>a</u> horses." (Plural nouns do, however, require definite articles: "I love <u>the</u> horses in the national park near my house.")
- **Noncount nouns** may not require articles: "Love conquers all," not "<u>A</u> love conquers all" or "<u>The</u> love conquers all."

(3) Using Other Determiners with Nouns

See C4

Determiners are words that function as <u>**adjectives**</u> to limit or qualify the meaning of nouns. In addition to articles, **demonstrative pronouns, possessive nouns and pronouns, numbers** (both **cardinal** and **ordinal**), and other words indicating *number* and *order* can function in this way.

1. **Demonstrative pronouns** (*this, that, these, those*) communicate

   - the relative nearness or fairness of the noun from the speaker's position (*this* and *these* for things that are *near, that* and *those* for things that are *far*): *this* book on my desk, *that* book on your desk; *these* shoes on my feet, *those* shoes in my closet.
   - the *number* of things indicated (*this* and *that* for *singular* nouns, *these* and *those* for *plural* nouns): *this* (or *that*) flower in the vase, *these* (or *those*) flowers in the garden.

2. **Possessive nouns** and **possessive pronouns** (*Ashraf's, his, their*) show who or what the noun belongs to: *Maria's* courage, *everybody's* fears, the *country's* natural resources, *my* personality, *our* groceries.

3. **Cardinal** numbers (*three, fifty, a thousand*) indicate how many of the noun you mean: *seven* continents. **Ordinal** numbers (*first, tenth, thirtieth*) indicate in what order the noun appears among other items: *third* planet. Use digits in both cardinal and ordinal numbers for units of measure.

4. Words other than numbers may indicate **amount** (*many, few*) and **order** (*next, last*) and function in the same ways as cardinal and ordinal numbers: *few* opportunities, *last* chance.

C2 Pronouns

Any English noun may be replaced by a **pronoun**. Pronouns ^{See A1.2} enable you to avoid repeating a noun over and over. For example, *doctor* may be replaced by *he* or *she, books* by *them*, and *computer* by *it*.

See A1.2

C3 Verbs

(1) Person and Number

Person refers to *who* or *what* is performing the action of the verb (for example, *myself, you,* or someone else), and **number** refers to *how many* people or things are performing the action (one or more than one). Unless you use the correct person and number in the verbs in your sentences, you will confuse your English-speaking audience by communicating meanings you do not intend.

See 11a4

(2) Tense

Tense refers to *when* the action of the verb takes place. One problem that many nonnative speakers of English have with English verb tenses results from the large number of **irregular verbs** in English. For example, the first-person singular present tense of *be* is not "I be" but "I am," and the past tense is not "I beed" but "I was."

See 6b

See 6a

Another problem occurs for some nonnative speakers of English when they use tenses that are more complicated than they need to be. Such speakers may do this because their native language uses more complicated tenses where English does not or because they are nervous about using simple tenses and "overcorrect" their verbs into complicated tenses.

Specifically, nonnative speakers tend to use **progressive** and **perfect** verb forms instead of **simple** verb forms. To communicate your ideas clearly to an English-speaking audience, choose the simplest possible verb tense.

(3) Auxiliary Verbs

Meaning is also communicated in English through the use of **auxiliary verbs** (also known as **helping verbs**), such as forms of the verbs *be* and *have* ("Julio *is taking* a vacation," "I *have been* tired lately.") and **modal auxiliaries** such as *would, should,* and *can* ("We *should conserve* more of our resources," "You *can succeed* if you try").

See A1.3

See A1.3

AUXILIARY VERBS

Only auxiliary verbs, not the verbs they "help," change form to indicate person, number, and tense.

We ~~have~~ had to ~~went~~ go downtown yesterday. (Only the auxiliary verb *had* should be in the past tense.)

Modal auxiliaries do not change form to indicate tense, person, or number.

(4) Negative Verbs

The meaning of a verb may be made negative in English in a variety of ways, chiefly by adding the words *not* or *does not* to the verb (is, *is not;* can ski, *can't* ski; drives a car, *does not* drive a car).

 CORRECTING DOUBLE NEGATIVES

A **double negative** occurs when the meaning of a verb is negated not just once but twice in a single sentence.

Henry doesn't have ~~no~~ any friends. (*or* Henry ~~doesn't~~ has ~~have~~ no friends.)

I looked for articles in the library, but there weren't none. (*or* I looked for articles in the library, but there weren't ~~none~~ any.)

C4 Adjectives and Adverbs

Adjectives and adverbs are words that modify (describe, limit, or qualify) other words.

(1) Position of Adjectives and Adverbs

Adjectives in English usually appear *before* the nouns they modify. A native speaker of English would not say, "*Cars red and black* are involved in more accidents than *cars blue or green*" but would say instead, "*Red and black cars* are involved in more accidents than *blue or green cars.*"

However, adjectives may appear *after* linking verbs ("The name seemed *familiar*"), direct objects ("The coach found them *tired* but *happy*."), and indefinite pronouns ("Anything *sad* makes me cry.")

Adverbs may appear *before or after* the verbs they describe, but they should be placed as close to the verb as possible: not "I *told* John that I couldn't meet him for lunch *politely*," but "I *politely told* John that I couldn't meet him for lunch" or "I *told* John *politely* that I couldn't meet him for lunch." When an adverb modifies an adjective or another adverb, it usually comes *before* the adjective or the adverb: "The essay has *basically sound* logic." However, adverbs may appear in a greater variety of positions than adjectives can.

(2) Order of Adjectives

A single noun may be modified by more than one adjective, perhaps even by a whole list of adjectives in a row. Given a list of three or four adjectives, most native speakers would arrange them in a sentence in the same order. If shoes are to be described as *green* and *big*, numbering *two*, and of the type worn for playing *tennis*, a native speaker would say "two big green tennis shoes." Generally, the adjectives that are most important in completing the meaning of the noun are placed closest to the noun.

ORDER OF ADJECTIVES

1. Articles (*a, the*), demonstratives (*this, those*), and possessives (*his, our, Maria's, everybody's*)
2. Amounts (*one, five, many, few*), order (*first, next, last*)
3. Personal opinions (*nice, ugly, crowded, pitiful*)
4. Sizes and shapes (*small, tall, straight, crooked*)
5. Age (*young, old, modern, ancient*)
6. Colors (*black, white, red, blue, dark, light*)
7. Nouns functioning as adjectives to form a unit with the noun (*soccer* ball, *cardboard* box, *history* class)

C5 Prepositions

In English, **prepositions** (such as *to, from, at, with, among, between*) give meaning to nouns by linking them with other words and other parts of the sentence. Prepositions convey several different kinds of information.

See A1.6

- Relations to **time** (*at* 9 o'clock, *in* 5 minutes, *for* a month)
- Relations of **place** (*in* the classroom, *at* the library, *beside* the chair) and **direction** (*to* the market, *onto* the stage, *toward* the freeway)

- Relations of **association** (go *with* someone, the tip *of* the iceberg)
- Relations of **purpose** (working *for* money, dieting *to* lose weight)

In some languages, prepositions may be used in quite different ways, may exist in forms quite different from English, or may not exist at all—and any of these situations may cause problems. However, speakers of languages with prepositions very similar to those in English—especially Romance languages such as Spanish, French, and Italian—may also have trouble with English prepositions because they may be tempted to translate prepositional phrases directly from their own language into English.

PREPOSITIONS IN IDIOMATIC EXPRESSIONS

Common Nonnative Speaker Usage	*Native Speaker Usage*
according *with*	according *to*
apologize *at*	apologize *to*
appeal *at*	appeal *to*
believe *at*	believe *in*
different *to*	different *from*
for least, *for* most	*at* least, *at* most
refer *at*	refer *to*
relevant *with*	relevant *to*
similar *with*	similar *to*
subscribe *with*	subscribe *to*

 Word Order

In English, word order is extremely important, contributing a good deal to the meaning of a sentence.

(1) Standard Word Order

Like Chinese, English is an "SVO" language, or one in which the most typical sentence pattern is "subject-verb-object." (Arabic, by contrast, is an example of a "VSO" language.) Deviation from the SVO pattern tends to confuse English speakers.

(2) Word Order in Questions

Word order in questions can be particularly troublesome for speakers of languages other than English, partly because there are so many different ways to form questions in English.

WORD ORDER IN QUESTIONS

1. To create a yes/no question from a statement using the verb *be,* simply invert the order of the subject and the verb:

   <u>Rasheem is</u> researching the depletion of the ozone layer.

   <u>Is Rasheem</u> researching the depletion of the ozone layer?

2. To create a yes/no question from a statement using a verb other than *be,* use a form of the auxiliary verb *do* before the sentence without inverting the subject and verb:

   <u>Does</u> Rasheem want to research the depletion of the ozone layer?

   <u>Do</u> Rasheem's friends want to help him with his research?

   <u>Did</u> Rasheem's professors approve his research proposal?

3. You can also form a question by adding a **tag question**—such as *won't he?* or *didn't I?*—to the end of a statement. If the verb of the main statement is *positive,* then the verb of the tag question is *negative;* if the verb of the main statement is *negative,* then the verb of the tag question is *positive:*

   Rasheem <u>is</u> researching the depletion of the ozone layer, <u>isn't he</u>?

   Rasheem <u>doesn't</u> intend to write his dissertation about the depletion of the ozone layer, <u>does he</u>?

4. To create a question asking for information, use **interrogative** words (*who, what, where, when, why, how*), and invert the order of the subject and verb (note that *who* functions as the subject of the question in which it appears):

   <u>Who is</u> researching the depletion of the ozone layer?

   <u>What is Rasheem</u> researching?

   <u>Where is Rasheem</u> researching the depletion of the ozone layer?

INDEX

Index

Index

Index

Index

Index

Index

Index

Index

Unique, 276
Units of measurement, abbreviating, 114
Until, 276
URL, 72, 110, 150–151, 155, 174, 239
Usage review, 268–277
Us and *we* before noun, 39
Used to, 275
Usenet, 153
Utility words, eliminating, 53–54
Utilize, 276

V

Varied sentences, writing, 49–52
Verbal phrase fragment, 22, 24
Verbal phrases, 265
  restrictive vs. nonrestrictive, 76–77
Verbals, 21, 261
Verb phrases, 261, 265
Verbs, 260–261, 281–282
  agreement between subjects and, 25–28
  auxiliary (helping), 261, 281–282
  base form of, 30
  correct usage of, 30–36
  to introduce source's words or ideas, 166
  inverted subject-verb order, 27
  irregular, 30–32, 281
  linking, 27, 42, 260
  main, 260, 265
  missing, supplying, 24
  mood and, 35–36
  negative, 282
  person and number in, 281
  regular, 30
  tenses, 33–35, 57, 281
  voice and, 36

words or phrases separating subject and, 52
Verb-subject-object (VSO) word order, 284
Vertical file, 145
Visuals
  checklist for, 237
  designing (checklist), 254
  effective, 232–237
  for speech, 253–254
Voice, 36. *See also* Passive voice
  shifts from active to passive, 57–58
Voice of the Shuttle (search engine), 150
Vowels in unstressed positions, 101
"VSO" language, 284

W

Wait for, wait on, 276
We and *us* before noun, 39
Weather, whether, 277
Web browser, 148–149, 174
Web Crawler (search engine), 149
Web page, 148
  designing, 237–241
  proofreading, 240
Web site, 148, 237
  bookmarking, 152, 172
  building, 237
  copyright and, 238
  creating (checklist), 241
  designing, 239
  determining legitimacy of (checklist), 155
  evaluation of, 154–156
  organizing information on, 238
  posting, 240
  useful, 157–164
Web site citation, Chicago style, 182

CREDITS